They Can't Be Loved Into Sobriety

Luis Velarde is a counselor and recovery coach who has over twenty-five years of experience coaching and training counselors, social workers and behavioral service professionals working in the juvenile justice system. He has provided counseling and recovery coaching to families and young adults struggling with substance abuse issues.

Luis attended the University of California, where he earned his B.A. and Masters Degree in Counseling. He later attended Columbia Pacific University where he earned his Doctorate in Health and Human Services. He is also a published author of the Strength-Based Recovery Coaching Tool Kit, Gang-free Zones and Zen and the Art of Retirement. *Dr. Velarde is a sought after speaker on issues relating to recovery coaching, youth at risk, and a trainer and member of:*

- Recovery Coach Network: Recovery Coach Trainer; counselor
- Recovery Coach International: member
- International Coaching Federation: member
- National Association of Alcoholism and Drug Abuse Counselors (NAADAC): member

ISBN-13: 978-1494361181

TABLE OF CONTENTS

ACKNOWLEDGEMENTS

I would like to acknowledge every family who has ever taken a brief detour in life as a result of their loved one's addiction and who understands the contents of this book because they have lived it or are living it. Over the past two years, I have commiserated with and interviewed families who were in agony because of their love one's addiction, and whose faces have shown me the hell they have endured.

I would like to thank everyone who contributed to the preparation of this book. They include first and foremost the students, of the various alternative high school where I served as counselor and principal, and who provided me with the up-close-and personal wisdom regarding gang and drug cultures.

I am grateful to my former colleagues at the Orange County Juvenile Hall facility, and most recently, the talented staff at New Beginnings and African American Family Services. Without their expert opinions, knowledge of the research and compassion for their young clients, this book would have been more difficult to write.

To my wife who has kept me balanced all these years, a tough job in itself. I am grateful for the time she sacrificed in sanitizing my expressed anger in this book and who allowed me the privilege of holding her during her darkest moments.

This book is also dedicated to all the men, women and organizations who have dedicated their lives to treating, understanding and advancing the research about this cunning, baffling, and powerful disease.

To the memory of Earnie Larsen and his work on addiction recovery. His books and recorded teachings have taught me simple, but important truths.

Finally, I give thanks to God, my Higher Power for keeping our son safe and our family together and sane. I thank Him for the time He has given me and for the privilege of sharing these pages with you.

A WORD ABOUT WORDING

"Our language is funny: a fat chance and slim chance is the same thing."
(My sixth grade teacher)

The term *drug* or *substance* is used throughout to define any natural herb or chemical including alcohol that is used for mood-altering purposes. The definition also extends to use (and abuse) of prescription or over-the-counter drugs for purposes other than those for which they are indicated or in a manner or in quantities other than directed. *(The International Classification of Diseases, 4th edition, the 9th revision, published by McGraw Hill for the World Health Organization.)*

I have taken the liberty to limit the use of the words addict or alcoholic as much as possible. Instead, I have interchangeably used the words child, teen, adolescent, kid, and loved one to demonstrate that they are all the same and that there can still be hope and family unity. A loved one is anyone who has become addicted or incarcerated as a result of substance use, and is in a parental, romantic, brotherly, or spiritual relationship with you.

Going deeper, a loved one is a person who you care about very much and whose faults you are willing to overlook, and for whom you would *reasonably* sacrifice anything, be it money, time, or both for his sake. I have emphasized the term reasonably because anything beyond that borders on enabling and co-dependency behaviors (treatment-speak for being up to your neck with your loved one's problems) and something I address in greater detail in this book.

As long as I'm clarifying structural issues, I have used the gender specific pronoun *he* throughout the book to avoid the awkward and redundant use of *he* or *she*, *him* or *her*.

I have also used the words *Creator, Great Spirit, Higher Power* and *God* interchangeably because all these terms refer to the same monotheistic deity, regardless of Western religious traditions. I've chosen God as my Higher

Power, and prayer as my way of communicating with Him.
It works for me. What you choose is up to you.

Disclaimer

The things which are written in this book have been witnessed by me and have also been confirmed by talking with parents and teens. I assume no responsibility for any event that may occur as a result of any parent using the enclosed information. This book is not meant to take the place of a doctor, psychiatrist, or counselor. If your teen or loved one is having serious substance abuse issues, you should consult a professional. The sole purpose of the information provided is to inform families that we need to go beyond unconditional love and move toward action when it comes to helping our addicted loved ones.

KEY TERMS

Abstinence: The complete stopping of the use of substances in all forms such as: potentially addictive prescription and over-the-counter medications; illicit or illegal drugs (natural or manufactured), and any other mood-altering substances.

Sobriety: To be sober beyond abstinence and learning the skills and lifestyle changes that will improve health, help solve life's problems, and allow for finding a sense of meaning in life.

Addiction: The use of alcohol, drugs or other compulsive disorders to get short-term relief from physical, psychological, or social problems and which in time makes those problems worse.

Treatment: Consists of specific activities recommended by and supervised by a doctor or therapist relating to the management of one's compulsive disorder or addiction.

Recovery: A process of change after treatment through which individuals improve their health and wellness, live a self-directed life, and continue striving to reach their full potential.

Aftercare: Continuing care following discharge from a clinic or hospital, and is at the stage where a client is able to function using a self-directed plan, which includes minimal interaction with a counselor, therapist, coach, case manager or sober peer.

Relapse: In recovery language, a relapse is when persons return to the use of an addictive substance of which they had previously established abstinence.

Enabling: Creating an atmosphere or situations that makes it easier for addictive persons to continue in the progression of their disease.

Codependency: A relationship in which a person with a compulsive disorder (in this case, addiction) is controlled or manipulated by another. Codependency can occur in any type of relationship, including family, work, friendship, or romantic.

HOW THIS BOOK CAME TO BE

"Help me Dad, I'm tired of running. I just want to rest."
(Cell phone message May, 2010)

To use a modified AA introduction, *"Hello, my name is Luis and I'm a recovering enabler."* Isn't that how all healing begins? There is nothing to writing. All you have to do is sit in front of your keyboard and bleed. This redone Ernest Hemingway quote has great meaning because writing this book has not been a walk in the park. Everyone has a story to tell regardless of where they are in life. Ours is about our son Dylan, a promising hockey goalie who went away to college in California and while there, hooked up with the wrong crowd and was brought up on drug charges, an ironic turn of events in light of that state's push for marijuana legalization. Through the efforts of our attorney and our son's clean record, we were able to transfer Dylan back to the Midwest where he was able to receive the necessary in-patient treatment and be close to family.

You read the title of this book correctly. Our substance using kids cannot be loved into sobriety; at least not exclusively. Substance-using kids can't hear the love messages parents keep sending out. They can be helped, but not through love and rescuing exclusively.

Two months after returning home and one stint at treatment, Dylan's drug use resumed which began a process that triggered a series of events that almost destroyed our family. This is also where my lessons in denial and co-dependency began and which taught me that something more was needed beyond loving, rescuing and hoping that somehow our son would grow out of it or that it's just a phase he was going through. Since the writing of this book, I have learned that it is not enough to rescue and provide for everything in a child's life and claim we are doing it in the name of unconditional love. That would be blatantly dishonest and, as you will learn through our experiences, harmful to a young person's development.

As a father, I needed to do something more than rescue Dylan each time he ran into numerous obstacles: school, sports, and life in general. I needed to come face-to-face with the reality that part of my life was also out of control. I had begun to internalize Dylan's drug problem and quickly slipped into a mode many fathers become mired in: rescuing, covering up, making deals, and throwing money at the problem (a common father response).

None of it worked. Was I too easy on the kid? Was I too hard? Was I unknowingly trying to relive my youth through his? At some point in his life, had I had failed him as a father? These questions had me bewildered. The pain of dealing with an endless cycle of disappointments and frustrations was indescribable.

It Is What It Is

You may be caught up in a similar situation. It may be a spouse, child, parent, someone in your family, or just a close friend who using and abusing alcohol and drugs. You may be feeling frustrated at the fact that you too have been stuck in blaming yourself exclusively for your loved one's sudden (or gradual) descent into that abyss that addiction is. You may be feeling as though, regardless of what you have tried, everything seems to be failing. You suddenly find you and your spouse at opposite ends of a metaphorical boxing ring, staring each other down and casting blame.

It is what it is. Some things are simply out of our control and there is little we can do to change them. The Alcoholics Anonymous Serenity Prayer comes to mind and how it can apply to families of addicted loved ones as well: *"God grant me the serenity to accept the things I cannot change; courage to change the things I can; and wisdom to know the difference."* Families need to understand those things we can control and those we can do little or nothing about. We must not make ourselves vulnerable to participation in any form of abuse be it physical, mental or spiritual.

If our ones continue to choose a path of destruction, we need to be strong enough to detach and exercise the freedom to choose not to be a part of it, or it will surely take us down along with them. That is what this book is about.

At the very least, this book will teach you how to let go of things we cannot change and begin taking ownership of those things we still can control: ourselves and how we react to a situation totally out of control. You will learn that one cannot respond rationally to irrational situations and why we become frustrated when logic and rationale do not work with alcoholics and addicts.

I hadn't intended this book for publication, but when I shared it with a colleague he insisted that it had something to say to families of adolescents who have used mind-altering chemicals and have paid a dear price for their choice; that young people everywhere were succumbing to a drug pandemic and wrecking the lives of millions of families. Part of my healing has been sharing an unflinching account of our experiences in the form of a book that can help families who may be suffering as a result of their child's substance use. It was something I needed to do for myself and it speaks from my heart in an effort to help families understand the challenges related to parenting an addicted child: denial, enabling, codependency, and self-blame. It was all something I already knew as a professional counselor, but was too close to the fray to acknowledge it until it was too late. By reading this book, you may discover as I did that you too might be just as addicted to your enabling behaviors as the addict in your life is to his or her drug induced manipulations.

Our story is no different than yours. It is interesting how the pain from the negative actions of our loved ones is universal; that disappointment and heartache rip at us all regardless of our stature or means.

They could be using different drugs, perhaps; from different cities; and treated in different rehabs; but the story is still the same nonetheless. No matter how educated or how many initials or titles we may have after our name, addiction and drug-fueled occurrences such as the ones our family endured can attack any family.

The Prodigal Son

There are some lessons about addiction and recovery that we can learn from the biblical story of the prodigal son: *The story is about a young man that treated his father as though he was dead and asked for his inheritance. He then set out for a faraway country, got in with the wrong crowd and spent all his money on a party lifestyle. The text says that when he had gotten enough of himself, and in tons of trouble, he had a moment of clarity and felt he had hit his own personal bottom and decided that the only way out of the pit he found himself in was in was up. He realized that he was powerless over his sinful lifestyle and that it would be better to be a servant in his father's house than to remain where he was and possibly perish. The only way to regain his life was to surrender it and put himself back under the control of his father. (Luke 15 paraphrased)*

If you go back and read this parable, you'll notice that the father does not go out and rescue his son. He does not give up hope, but instead patiently waits for his son to have his fill of the mess he has been in and prays to God that his son returns safely. When the son makes a decision (on his own) to return, the father is not judgmental or critical of his son. Instead the father is loving and supportive.

This parable could very well be about our loved one's addiction and recovery. Though we all continue to fight for our children's well-being, ultimately they will make all the choices; right or wrong, and they will live and die with or without our involvement. Some will be taken from us by that silent enemy, and there is little a father can do to prevent, cure or control it.

So there we sit, blaming ourselves for the wrong choices our loved ones have made. Each of us looking out in the distance; waiting for our prodigal son to return with nothing to do but keep our fingers crossed and our homes open to hope.

Although our story doesn't have a fireworks-in-the-sky happy ending, we feel blessed that our son Dylan is getting his life back, moments of struggle notwithstanding. It is my hope your story will end happily as well. It is also my hope that this book serves as a model and inspiration to families who have found themselves in a similar situation.

OH NO! NOT MY KID

"Even the strongest love in the world cannot cure addiction"
(Earnie Larsen)

Imagine coming home early from work and finding that your bedroom dresser has been ransacked. How many times have you seen a wall in your home with a hole so big you could shoot a basketball through it, and without anyone knowing how it got there? Try to envision the hordes of young strangers invading your basement and using it as a public restroom and community crash pad. Imagine further, finding your credit card missing only to find out weeks later that someone has depleted your account. How many times have you been awakened in the middle of the night by a phone call from a jail in a sketchy part of town, informing you that they have your teen locked up? And finally, how often have you been lied to, cheated and manipulated by the very person you once taught how to ride a bicycle?

Does this illustrate any part of your story? It is interesting how the pain, disappointment, and heartache from the negative actions of our teens rip at us all regardless of family stature and means. As you will learn through reading of our own experience, the person struggling with substance use is not the only one affected by addiction. Loved ones also face fears, sadness, anger, and co-dependency issues when made aware of a loved one's drug use.

I'll get right to the point. Like any family, our lives had been made miserable by addiction's grip on our son, Dylan. The pressures that his addiction placed on us was unbearable as we tried to find ways to *fix* the addict we loved so dearly, not knowing that addiction couldn't be fixed. We were being held hostage and at the mercy of something we couldn't control, and with language and terms we didn't fully understand.

We used up a great deal of precious resources (time, energy, money) often short-changing our other loved ones in the process, while all the time Dylan stood still, seemingly oblivious to, or unimpressed by our frantic efforts to stop his freefall. We tightened up on discipline, but that didn't work.

We tried compromising and were ripped off each time. We tried to reason with him out of love and concern for his welfare, not realizing that rationalizing rarely works with addicted persons. Love and concern for our pleas were no longer in Dylan's priorities and was unable to keep promises and honor his agreements.

These are all typical addictive behaviors. With addicts and alcoholics, their rational and reasoning capabilities become easily hijacked by their drug of choice.   Families caught in this situation fail to understand that our well-meaning rational responses do little to change an irrational situation so we continue to blame ourselves for the mistakes of our loved ones and bury our heads in the sand; tired, disappointed, and frustrated.

Addiction often causes these dynamic; a family consumed with trying anything that will work, and a loved one unwilling, uninterested or unmotivated to change his behavior. How does one love a substance abuser into sobriety? Better yet, a resistant one? The truth is you can't. Something has to change. You can wait for him to hit *rock bottom*, but that could backfire on the whole family in negative ways. You see, no one really knows what that rock bottom may be and I'm told it's different for each addict; and what if rock bottom is death? The point behind all this is that many more young people are doing drugs and alcohol and can't stop, and why not? Many factors play into this. If they could simply *just say no* as Nancy Reagan once suggested their addictions would end and there would be little need for counselors and treatment facilities. But many just can't.

IT'S A BEAUTIFUL DAY IN THE NEIGHBORHOOD...2013

"Love without boundaries is not love."
(James Lehman)

60 Minutes ran a story in May of 2008 discussing a new generation of young people   born between 1980 and 1995 known as *Millennials*. According to experts interviewed, millennials are also being referred to as the *coddled generation;* children who have been raised by doting parents once known as Baby Boomers, Generation X'ers and today, Helicopter moms. Collectively or individually, they have been selling the fantasy to their kids that they can be anything they want, not so much for their hard work, but for just showing up, Not true? Then check out the boxes of trophies, plaques, and ribbons in their closets.

Millennials want to have everything and they want it now. They were raised with the narcissistic expectation that they will always win no matter what. Millennials are seen as enormously clever, bright and many are just plain Incorrigible. Many believe they are immune to life's consequences. They are tech savvy, they multi-task well, and the many electronic devices they carry are now an extension of their bodies. If a millennial gets a lower grade than expected in school, the kid immediately shoots home a text message, and by 3:30 that afternoon a teacher is in the office defending the grade the child *earned* and a parent insisting the grade be changed to one the child *deserves*. What does all this have to do with the substance abuse issues in this country? Read on.

Now, I'm not trying to paint all millennials, baby boomers GenXers and helicopter moms as wrong and hopeless. Many have their heads in the right place. Good for them. But the point I am trying to make is that many come from parents who smoked pot in their younger days and today have an open attitude about alcohol and drug use. Not true?

Then explain why the recent national 62% poll rating to legalize pot once and for all has drastically shifted overnight. No mystery here. Many millennials have grown up with parents who, while not drug addicts, were very open and honest about their years of herbal indulgence and chemical experimentation and many of whom had been cross-addicted with Valium and alcohol (*mother's little helpers*). When it came to drugs, alcohol and sex, nothing was forbidden. Everything was out in the open: how drugs made you feel, which ones were good or laced, and the best music to listen to while stoned: anything by Pink Floyd especially *comfortably Numb*; *Sparks* by The Who; *Crystal Ship* by The Doors; *Dazed and Confused* by Led Zeppelin to name a few.

Today however, mom's new little helper has become Adderall (a central nervous system stimulant) not to treat ADHD, but to help them get through the day. What makes Adderall attractive to mothers is its ability to help them cope with stress, feel energized and extremely focused, and to lose weight. Feeling like a *supermom* and weight loss has now become primary motives for abuse.

Synthetic Cannabinoids

Synthetics or *legal bud* as it is called by kids today, can still be easily purchased in "Head Shops", music stores and over the internet in thirty states, but is rapidly being made illegal by the DEA. As if parents did not already have enough to worry about, with over 75 percent of America's adolescents under age eighteen have reported using alcohol, and half have smoked marijuana or tried other drugs, now there is synthetic marijuana -- a product legally marketed as *herbal incense* that will reportedly get you high if you smoke it. Young people flock to legal bud because it's easier to obtain and it doesn't trigger a positive result on a urine drug test and are marketed as being "100% organic" insinuating that they are natural and completely safe.

Nothing in the drug world is fully "natural". Synthetic marijuana is a mixture of dried leaves from traditional herbal plants, but laced with chemicals developed in laboratories. Studies are beginning to show that Synthetic Cannabinoids are dangerous to the nervous system and very little is still known of its toxicity.

It's a Family Affair

It comes to no surprise then, that most young millennials today who are experiencing drug and alcohol issues don't want help or think they don't need treatment. This may be because most drugs are legal and openly marketed. Or it may be that their addiction history may not be of a sufficient duration to have caused them serious enough consequences, and the parental protection they have received has kept them insulated from many of those consequences. Couple that with a family's minimization or blindness to the early signs of drug and alcohol use, and one can see the surmountable problems that can result when it becomes too late to intervene. It is only when an adolescent's drug use leads to the *collateral consequences* such as law enforcement involvement, jail, an auto accident, a near death experience, or a court-mandate, that intervention becomes a hard-faced reality. It is now a documented fact that the majorities of adolescents who come to treatment do so by way of a hospital's emergency ward, the juvenile justice system, or have been court-mandated to attend. Almost 80 percent of young people in the juvenile justice system are there because of alcohol or drug-related crimes, and over three quarters of all incidences of teen violence (rape, homicides, and assaultive behaviors) have been tied to alcohol and drugs use.

If you happen to be one of the thousands of parents who have a loved that is on a *crash and burn* course through the use of drugs and alcohol, and if you are fighting the battle of your life, then this book is for you.

A NATION ON DRUGS

"All truth passes through four stages. First, it is ridiculed and made fun of. Second, it is violently opposed. Third, it is accepted as being self-evident, and fourth it becomes law."

(Friedrich Nietzsche)

The total cost of drug abuse in the U.S. last year exceeded $400 billion dollars, mostly in health care and crime related costs. And those are just the statistics that describe a snippet of the problem. Nothing is said about the suffering: addiction and its far-reaching personal, social, and economic costs to families. *(National Center on Addiction and Substance Abuse, "Adolescent Substance Abuse, 2011.)*

Addiction has many faces and respects no one. It is an equal opportunity destroyer. Once addiction has gained access to a life, it refuses to leave without a fight, and it won't fight fairly. It is insidious and may strike all at once or it may slither in slowly. Addiction is never satisfied. After it has ruined a life, ended a career, destroyed someone's health or put someone in the hospital (or the grave), it still wants more. Larry King of CNN fame once called it *America's new, silent epidemic.*

So why do many kids use alcohol and drugs, and why can't they just stop? I have three simple, but accurate reasons why our teens may be prone to alcohol and drug use:

1. We are a nation on drugs; hooked on porn, video games and pot. We use because we choose. We celebrate using. Think about it. In Colorado and Washington State marijuana is now legal for recreational use. In California, Alaska, Arizona and seventeen other states when accompanied with a prescription, it's called *medicine.* I don't have the data to prove it, but it is generally scientifically accepted that Americans rely on *cannabis* more than any other people on earth.

   The term cannabis is used here because in today's medical marijuana market it is no longer necessary to roll a joint and inhale pot to benefit from the effects of THC.

Today, with a prescription that can be obtained in thirty minutes for fifty dollars, THC found in cannabis can be obtained from a dispensary in tincture form for teas, in cookies, salad dressing, chocolate bars, Rice Krispie bars, lollipops and a form of chewing gum. The justification given by proponents of legalization is that inhaling pot is *old school,* harmful to one's lungs, and draws too much negative attention to the user. It's much safer and more fun to munch on a chocolate bar laced with TCH as we sit on a corner waiting for the next bus.

People use drugs because drugs work. They eliminate pain and enhance pleasure. The commercials we see on television make this assertion very clear. Do you have a headache? Take a painkiller. Are your kids hassling you? Take a Xanax or Valium. Feeling tired? Grab a can of Red Bull. Want to relax? Have a cocktail or smoke a prescription joint. Can't Sleep? Take Ambien. Are you a little depressed? Cymbalta has the answer. Problems with your sex drive? I think you get the picture. One reason our society has become so dependent on drugs is that we are constantly hearing about how great drugs are. In a study conducted by the University of Pittsburg (Feb. 2008) on the media's effects on drug and alcohol on adolescents, it stated that the media has a pronounced influence on young people's risk behaviors. The article cited: the average adolescent is exposed to approximately 84 references to drug use per day and 591 references per week, or 30,732 references per year.

Adolescents are bombarded on a daily basis with messages that suggest that one doesn't ever have to feel bad about anything; that no matter what ails you, there's a drug for it.

2. Beyond the obvious peer pressure and *forbidden fruit* curiosity, adolescents use drugs because they like it and what the drug of choice does for them. The reward centers in the brain give them instantaneous, but temporary pain-free pleasure, on demand, anytime they want it. It's what keeps them coming back. Not only do

drugs work, they work quickly and reliably. Young people self-medicate to feel comfortable in uncomfortable situations, making social interactions easier (boomer term: *social lubricants*). To a shy, inhibited kid, drugs provide a new found confidence. And finally, for the lonely outcast; the kid with terminal zits who nobody wants to associate with, drugs provides him a new social group: other users. And that's how it is. Drugs provide an escape from whatever a young person wants to escape. The sad part however, is that with increased use, the reward centers in the brain shut down and increased use is now demanded for stabilization purposes, and no longer for pleasure.

Just like with their adult role models, kids want to feel good and be free of stress and pain, but the problem is more developmentally severe for young people. Adolescents who use alcohol or drugs usually begin using in middle school which is the worst possible time to start, for many reasons. One being that in order for young people to develop normally, they must first learn to use their emotions and reasoning capabilities to give them energy and direction for problem solving.

The problem becomes one of the frontal cortexes of the brain, the part that controls rational thinking have not fully developed and when they become blocked or altered through chemical use, dependency patterns begin to develop and rational thinking becomes limited or is no longer possible. This is where a young person's life begins to unravel. Supporting this theory are recent studies that point to the younger the *age of first use*, the greater the struggle for mental, emotional and physical development. When a person begins ingesting substances at a very early age, their brain's chemistry becomes greatly altered. Drugs, including marijuana, can quickly wreak havoc on a young, developing brain precisely at a time the brain is supposed to be maturing. The University of Cincinnati study on Adolescent Brain Function (2008) noted that consistent use of marijuana by adolescents reduces IQ by six points, which is why "the age of first use" has now become a critical question being asked of young people when enrolling in treatment. Studies are now showing that the younger the age of use the greater the struggle for development. For boys it's 11.5 years and for girls, 12.5 years. (*U.S. Dept. of Justice, 2006*). So, one can see how using drugs can severely harm an adolescent's physical, emotional, social, and mental development.

3. Medical experts point to addiction as a brain disease that causes several abnormal chemistry reactions or responses in the brain that makes it easy for young people to become addicted. They point to psychosocial, physiological and neurological models to explain a person's inclination to use alcohol and other drugs. A combination of all or any of these patterns can be causal effects of course, such as a child having a genetic predisposition to vulnerability for addiction, but let's get real.

There are millions of kids from alcoholic backgrounds that are not predisposed to alcoholism. There are a million others like myself who cut a wide swath of debauchery across the seventies and was never affected. So we shouldn't make the generalization that young people who use alcohol and drugs are genetic prisoners (*he took after his uncle*), or victims of environmental influences. Speaking for myself, I would never wish my seventies upbringing in East Los Angeles on anyone, but I wouldn't trade it for the world. So there must be other factors more critical and which contribute greater to the use of alcohol and other drugs.

IT'S STILL ALL ABOUT CHOICE

We are all creatures of choice; free will. We're all very intelligent and good-looking and all that. Animals, on the other hand, are by in large driven by instincts. If they feel hunger, they eat. If they get the instinct to procreate, they breed, and anywhere they please. With humans, choice come great responsibility, and with this responsibility there come great consequences. History and the Bible are full of examples. One step in the wrong direction can lead to ultimate grief. Thumbing through my son's J.K. Rowling's <u>Harry Potter and the Chamber of Secrets,</u> I stumbled upon the simple answer to the question of choice and a great segue to the topic of choice as it relates to substance abuse: *"It is our choices, Harry, that show what we truly are, far more than our abilities."*

Outside of mental disorders, or other traumatic emotional wounds (child sexual abuse, rape, incest or some other heinous form of abuse), young people, for the most part, make a conscious choice to use mind altering substances. They did not begin using because they were raised in a dysfunctional family and lacked direction. Heck, most of us are born into some form of dysfunction, and the view that drug use was caused by a lack of will power, low intelligence or poor strength of character is

just plain wrong. Young people don't begin using because they are being raised in a strict environment with parents who hold them accountable to tough standards which results in teen rebellion. And for sure, they didn't begin using because their parents became separated or divorced. To some kids, if the home is devoid of security, love and joy, divorce is often a welcomed relief. Many kids, I'm guessing, would probably sigh, *"Whew, finally!"* I think I've made my point. Just like adults, young people use because in bad times, drugs make them feel better, and when they feel great, drug use makes them feel even greater.

What about all free time kids enjoy these days. Alcohol and other drug use by young people have been found to occur most often between the hours of 3 p.m. and 7 p.m. prior to parents coming home from work. Today they say that most adolescent crimes also occur between 3 and 7 p.m. No surprise there. So what does that say about the importance of after school activities in the deterrence or prevention of drugs and alcohol use among teens? *(Office of Juvenile Justice and Delinquency, 2012)*

I stand by my assertion that beyond severe genetic or psycho-medical reasons, young people today for the most part become addicted through the poor choices they make. They simply like the feeling drugs provide and they keep coming back for more until after habitual use their brain becomes chemically altered and their rational thinking capabilities become sabotaged. It's as if something in their brain has thrown a metaphorical switch, and they lose all control over their habit and their ability to self-manage. The young person has now become a defensive, irrational, manipulative, and chronically angry stranger who has compromised all values and ethics that you instilled in him for his drug of choice.

Whether they sniff it, smoke it, inject it, eat it, or put it where the sun doesn't shine, the results are all the same: *addiction*. It's a simple formula with anyone, but quicker with adolescents: continued use becomes abuse, and continued abuse becomes addiction.

With a little help, and support, changing our loved ones drug use and abuse is something parents can do something about, but when the disease evolves into addiction, change then becomes a task for treatment the experts. Substance use and abuse is voluntary. And there are several ways that we can treat a problem of habitual choice: *tough love* and following through on the boundaries we have set and getting to the help they need quickly.

Let's separate some terms here. Unconditional love means that we love someone without any reservations. In alcohol and substance abuse, tough love means that while we still love a person unconditionally, we do not always love or like or respect their behavior. Sometimes we need to let them fall on their faces and feel the consequences of their choices. Enabling a person may be the very thing that will hinder them from getting clean and sober. I contend that if someone in your home has made a conscious decision to use and abuse drugs or alcohol and has not become addicted to the point they need medical help, they can, with strong family support, take positive steps, and seek professional help, and choose once again to not use.

ABOUT OUR SON

"Come on in she said. I'll give you shelter from the storm."
(Bob Dylan)

Looking back, there have only been a few moments in my life when I've felt like a successful parent. Encouraging and watching Dylan become a great hockey goalie, and getting him into college, are the few bright spots that quickly come to mind. There are a few other hazier, great moments that I go to from time to time, usually when I'm alone fishing.

You could say our son Dylan is an *"everyteen."* Come to think of it, he could be yours. He is a handsome, young man of eighteen entering his first year of college and who loves to snowboard in winter and surf in summer. He became quite proficient at surfing during his first California summer while away at college. You might say he was on his way to becoming a natural.

During my short visits to see him, we spent some great hours together on the beach; me up on the sand by an old, deserted lifeguard station munching on a piece of string cheese and crackers, and he down below waxing his board. I can still hear a faint *"Woohoo!"* in the distance as he aims his board directly into a thundering wave. By dusk, it becomes hard to get him out of the water because the more he faces each swell, the better he gets and the longer he wants to stay. If you could see him kneeling on his board in his black wet suit, waiting for the next wave, you would swear you were looking at a frolicking seal. Life was as about as good as it could ever get for the two of us.

Dylan is a tall and slender young man with a deep brown tan from hours in the sun. His thick black hair has begun to grow into dreadlocks. He wears a thick, hemp rope necklace around his neck with a polished glass amulet for a lucky charm.

His long, dark legs protrude through his oversized cargo pants, and his faded Pink Floyd tank top reveals his equally long, lanky arms.

When he can't find his old pair of Van's beach shoes he wears a beat-up pair of sandals, exposing his long and narrow brown feet to the world. He considers himself a borderline vegetarian, nature lover, and spiritual. He is one who sees the human landscape differently than anyone else. His green-blue eyes slant down and his smile can light up a room. He is also a lover of music: Dub Step, Reggae, Beatles (post *Revolver*), Radiohead, Michael Franti, Pink Floyd, and some (out-of-the-mainstream) Santana world music. And that is our son.

What's the point of my telling you all this? How can both the loveable, communicative, happy-go-lucky young man, whose diapers I once changed, and the manipulative, self-destructive addict be one and the same? How can such a creative being abandon that warm, friendly, unique personality that made him my son, take up residence in an empty shell that is now the addict? And how can any parent make sense of it all?

We had always suspected something unrelated to studies was going on with Dylan even before he left for college, but he was really a good kid and seemed to be well adjusted. By the end of the first semester, he began to distance himself. He rarely phoned home, and when he did, the communications were short and uneasy. He was not working, but admitted he wasn't looking for work very hard. He would not talk much and we did not know what was really going on in his life. We prayed for him every day, every night, and many times in between. One evening, out of the blue, I listened to an anxious phone message from Dylan saying he needed help; that he had been arrested: *"I'm tired of running, dad. I just want to lie down and rest."*

But Our Teen is Different! (Questionnaire)

Circle yes or no to the following questions. If your answers are more yes than no, you may want to consider contacting a mental health provider, doctor or the local law enforcement agency.

1. Yes   No   Do you think that your teens could *not* possibly be involved in drugs or alcohol even though you realize that they are exposed to it in their schools?

> Most parents prefer to believe that it is someone else's child that has a problem. Drugs and alcohol are everywhere. No family is immune.

2. Yes   No   Do you think that because your teen gets good grades that he or she is immune to an addiction problem?

> Statistics show that all kinds of kids across the academic and social spectrum have drug and alcohol problems.

3. Yes   No   Do you feel guilty checking up on who your teen's friends are and where they go?

> It is your duty as a parent to know where your teen is, what he is doing, and whom he is doing it with.

4. Yes   No   Do you consider your teen's room as their "private space" and that you must respect it.

> Unless your teen is paying rent and utilities for his or her "private space", you have every right and a duty to search whatever is necessary when you suspect your teen is using drugs or alcohol. Kids have very clever hiding places for their stash.

5. Yes   No   Do you hide suspicious information about your teen from your spouse or other family members?

> Don't play games! The best way to fight a loved one's addiction is to lay everything out in the open, be honest.

6. Yes   No   Do you and your spouse blame each other for

your teen's problems.

> Playing the blame game is counterproductive and wastes everyone's time. Parents must deal with the problem together; forming a united front.

7. Yes   No   Have things or money mysteriously

disappeared from your home?

> Drugs are expensive. If you suspect, investigate! It is not uncommon for a person using substances to steal from their own family to support their habit.

8. Yes No   Does your teen carry around a bottle of eye drops?

> Red eyes may be a symptom of drug use. Be suspicious.

9. Yes No   Have you found empty pill bottles, tin foil wrappers

in the trash can in your teen's bedroom?

> Wake up! This is a sure sign that someone in your home is using. Investigate it ASAP. Tin foil is used for various reasons: free-basing crack or as a straw or makeshift pipe for marijuana consumption.

10. Yes   No   Have you noticed sudden changes in your
teen's grades, attitude, personality, friends?

> Be concerned if your teen becomes a different person. Personality changes, loss of respect, changes in friends, and style of dress can be a sign that your teen is drug involved.

(Source: Al-Anon)

LETTER TO MY SON: Week Two

Dear son:

We have had difficulty getting information as to where you have been sent after your arrest. We have been terrified and frustrated, and for good reason. We had to make countless long distance calls and spend eternity on the Internet trying to find you in the system, but couldn't. The *system*, can you believe that? I can't believe I'm speaking this way. Finally, after four days, someone from Orange County decided to enter a batch of names into their computer all at once and we were able to locate you. This has certainly been a surreal experience for all of us, especially you, an eighteen year-old college kid who has never been in jail.

Up front, let me get this off my chest. To this day, my first reaction has been shock and tremendous anger over this whole crisis caused by your irresponsible decision. It has now been followed by a deep pain. You broke some pretty serious laws, son. What has me baffled is that you made a conscious decision to break them. Drugs became your best friend and your personal *default* system for solutions to your problems. But choices made through addiction are still conscious decisions nonetheless and being *ripped* (to use your term) is no excuse for the crime you have committed and the sorrow and pain you have now brought upon yourself and our family.

I am not writing you to beat you up over this. You are probably doing that to yourself already. All the lecturing and *I told you so's* will have little effect.

You would just shut down and both of us wouldn't want that to happen. Just know that I am thoroughly pissed and deserve to be.

I just want you to understand my anger. I feel angry, hurt and used at the choices you made that got you where you are today. I am hurt by your foolish actions;

disappointed in your lack of self-control; and I feel used in that you not only conned sympathy and money from people most close to you, but also manipulated trust from those who believed in you and provided safe shelter for you while away at college. You lied to those who shouldn't have trusted you had they known of your drug problem. I am deeply saddened by the fact that you will be spending your nineteenth birthday locked up in a cage like an animal.

I am also feeling guilty because I went out of my way to do everything for you and, looking back, maybe I shouldn't have. It's been quite a rude awakening, being out-smarted on every level by someone who I taught how to fish. I am slowly beginning to understand that perhaps all the denial, dishonesty and manipulations were not a trait of your personality, but that it was more a very common side effect of your substance use and an addiction that had a life of its own. How else could you do the things you did to yourself and betray those that loved and supported you?

If you had been a stranger and had displayed all these characteristics to me, I would have run as fast as possible away from you. But what kind of a father runs away from his own son? I am still trying to wrap my head around all this.

Now you've earned some time to think and hopefully have come to the harsh realization that your addiction-induced judgment hurt you and our family in different ways. I just hope that you come out of this a wiser man from this experience.

Call me crazy, but I believe that God has been sending you warnings that you might've not heard or gone ignored by you earlier. So now son, God has sent you his loudest, *"What you reap you shall sow"* warning in real time in hopes that this time it will get your attention. Maybe through this experience you will finally see the consequences of your actions more clearly and finally get the help you need.

For now, I think it's best that we all take this time to think, cool off and digest everything that has happened. Then, I believe that with a little work, some of the anger and frustration we're all experiencing will dissipate. We haven't given up on you, son. My expression of anger is just my way of saying that although we are disappointed, we still care and will be with you through it all. Above all else, you are our son and we love you unconditionally. I'll write more once we find out where you are being processed and have settled in a more permanent location.

Until we fish again, be at peace where you are at.

Love, Dad.

California Dreamin'

"Changing is what people do when they have no options left."
(Oscar Wilde)

I'm up very early these days, but that seems to be the only time my head is clear. Today is special, however. I'm in California or as the kids say, *Cali*, and soon I'll be visiting my son, not on the beach or what was his college campus, but this time in jail. These have been some spirit-crushing days for our family and it seems like I have made a quantum leap from just plain crazy to insane. But I guess that's part of all this madness. I look over my laptop from this modest motel room by the beach and as I survey all the beautiful palm trees, I think in an almost audible tone, *"This is a beautiful place."* I'm from here, born and raised. I used to teach at a community college just down the road back in the eighties. Nothing has really changed except the traffic has become unbearable. I've been told that the freeway to the facility where my son is being held is the roughest. No matter. The weather is always great in Cali and its visiting day.

We find parking and my wife and I walk the two long blocks that it takes to get to the Orange County Jail's main reception area and work our way over to where the lines are already wrapping around the outside of the building. Shifting uncomfortably on my feet, I look around at my surroundings. To my left is the County Child Protection Center that, I guess, houses children of abusive parents. Funny, how it's always the children who get locked up for the sins of their parents. Next to it is the juvenile hall facility. To the very far right is the county dog pound, and in the middle of this entire surreal layout is the building where we will be visiting our son.

We are directed to register at two makeshift tables at the front of the entrance where two young men in orange jumpsuits with the initials CWP on their backs (presumably, County Work Program), are diligently flipping through a two-inch thick printout containing lists of names and numbers of the inmates being visited that day. Once our son's name has been located and our ID's checked, we are directed to store our metal belongings and jackets in the rickety, vintage W.W.II lockers where they will be left at the mercy of strangers.

It is now 10:00 a.m. and I'm getting restless. The temperature has risen to seventy-eight degrees and will cap off at around eighty-five. I have mentally counted an array of fifty somber faces in the line we are in and by the look of things I can tell that we're in for a rough day. I think of our son and how he may be getting along inside and mumble to myself, *"This is not going to be like the hockey camp visits of past years."* You see, our son is a baby-faced, lanky, eighteen year old who, up until now, has never even gotten a traffic violation and who finds himself locked up with fully grown, streetwise criminals. Each day that he is in there, he will be coming down from his drug use, where the reality of his crime will hit him hard; all at once. He will undoubtedly become increasingly paranoid and fearful, and react in ways that may jeopardize his physical and mental well-being. I suddenly shake those thoughts from my head as I feel an understanding squeeze of my wife's hand. I look at her eyes, which have become quite puffy from crying. I helplessly nudge her to move up so as to close the gap in line as we prepare to be patient.

The people at the head of the line have been here since dawn. Others seem pretty casual about this whole experience as they simply wolf down bags of potato chips and chat.

One poor soul in his fifties sits in his electric wheelchair, sadly staring at the narrow sidewalk, making his own sacrifice in his own way and perhaps, not for the first time. By the look of his faded tattoo on his forearm, a too-familiar religious cross; and a blue teardrop tatooed beneath his left eye, I begin to imagine: *"This tired old guy must be a casualty of some bygone gang war."* My wife stands quietly, wide-eyed, fearful that she is in a house of horrors, as this is nothing like her beloved Midwest. I just grit my teeth and politely look away.

I catch a glimpse of a duty officer signaling us to move up and finally enter the building. As if in a set of a social science fiction movie set, we walk through a gray cylindrical metal detector. An Orwellian voice bellows, *"Please step back and deposit all metal objects in the basket by the doorway,"* reminding me that I had not stored my watch. This is all done in English, Spanish, and Southeast Asian, by the way.

The lobby is hot and crowded. In one corner of the lobby is that same disabled man scooting his wheelchair closer to the only electric fan in the lobby. Someone across from us is trying to open a bag of chips for his son, while a woman to my left is bending over; exposing an over-sized tattooed breast as she calmly cleans the yellow-orange Cheetos stains of her child's shirt. She looks in my direction as if sensing that someone is staring, and I sheepishly look the other way.

I pull out sheets of printed materials from my folder; stuff I had downloaded about what will become valuable information when visiting our son: prison schedules; when visits are allowed, the times, and the hours for making money deposits for inmate use in the commissary.

As I look up from my folder, I become aware of the sad faces in the crowd. We smile at a few and they return the gesture. We try to set our middle class prejudices aside and realize that, in their own way, they are all good families. They love someone in this place enough to wake up at dawn, drive long distances just to stand in long sweaty lines for a brief opportunity to visit a loved one. They come from many different walks of life. Some of the visitors in the room are fanning themselves with their forms and other paperwork, and by looking at them, one can tell they are the poorest of the poor. Others, though few, seem wealthy; dressed straight out of Nordstrom's and behave as if they are above it all. Their arms are crossed as if they have been summoned to another boring PTA meeting and one can easily tell by the way they shift in their chairs that they have never seen (or smelled) poverty. There are lots of moneyed people in Orange County. But when it is all sorted out, none of us is exempt.

This morning, like it or not, West coast, East coast, Midwest, rich or poor, we have all come together as one, in one room, to share our only common bond: a visit with a loved one.

A LETTER TO EVERY FIRST TIME OFFENDER

To Whom It May Concern:

Hello, my name is Dylan, a drug-related offender and the person whom this story is about. Welcome to what we lovingly refer to as Hotel *California*. Let me talk to you frankly from the inside of this stark, cold place where you will undoubtedly wind up if you continue on the roller coaster ride you have been on. What I'm offering you is a private tour and a firsthand look at what I have experienced these last few months.

About two-thirds of the inmates in this place are pretrial detainees who have been charged, but have not been convicted of a crime. Of those two-thirds there are the short timers like me who serve less than a year or who do not have the money to post bail. The other third of the population I would guess are either gang affiliated, or waiting to be transported to the state prison. Many others are undocumented inmates referred to as "*Border Brothas*" waiting to be shipped back to Tijuana, Mexico. There is nothing much to do to pass the time here except play cards, Spades usually. Then there's scrabble, or we can watch TV or figure out ways to "get over the system." Scary? You bet it is.

Many inmates have relayed to me in our weekly group sessions that they have regretted nothing regarding their drug-fueled arrests. They are grateful, in fact for the lesson they have learned and all they have been through. What is strange about lessons gone unlearned is that for many, this is their second and even third trip to the joint. As for me, the truth is that I do regret my past; very much so.

I have become saddened and disgusted over what I did. My addiction sucked to no end and I am sorry a lost a small chunk of my life while addicted. I wish I had not put my family through all this, and I wish that I would have done the right thing by staying in school. But it is what it is and I'm young enough to hopefully recapture a lot of what I lost and take advantage of what lies ahead.

But, enough about me. Let's begin our tour. From the moment you were arrested and sent to the county jail for processing, your life changed. Now, all the rules have changed and you must play by new ones. You entered a different world; a surreal country-within-a-country. There are only two kinds of rules in the joint: 1) the rules of the federal, state or county penal system; and 2) the rules of the inmate community. Not all jails and prisons are the same, but most play by similar rules. I think you are beginning to get the picture. Now it is time for some serious institutional life lessons:

- *You are now a number without a name. There are no civil rights in the joint. When things begin to get harsh, bite your tongue. This is not a place where you can lodge complaints. Take your county-issued overalls, thin wool blanket and pillow (if you're lucky enough to get a pillow) and move on. Keep your mouth shut. Nothing you can say will make the situation any better and it might even make things worse. Scary? You bet it is. Read on.*

- *Do your best to take care of your hygiene while in the joint. Certain hygiene items that you once took for granted may not be available or won't be as good.*

- *Begin to find out how each system works; the official one and the unofficial one (inmate community). If there is an official rule book for that facility, read it. You can be punished for breaking a rule that you didn't even know existed. Breaking the rules will not only piss off personnel, but inmates as well. It makes life harder for everyone. Ignorance of the rules is no defense and solid information is power.*

- *Hang with people of your own kind. In the joint, people are usually separated by race or gang affiliation anyway, but still make sure you are with your own people. It is not so much about racial discrimination, but more about safety. When in Rome, get with the Romans. Showing allegiance to your race is crucial to your survival in the joint.*

  Today, more than ever, the population of biracial inmates has grown significantly. If this is you, here are some tips: A biracial inmate cannot survive in the joint if one week he states he's black and another week he claims to be white or Latino. It simply means that whichever race you have claimed, seek that group out first, before you are approached and made to decide on the spot. There are places where you can be friendly with people of other races, but jail isn't one of them. As a general rule, blacks, Latinos, Asians and whites all look after their own. This isn't the time or place to be liberal or colorblind.

- *Never trust anyone. That goes for guards, prison officials, and others in your inmate community. If someone is being nice to you, ask yourself, "What's in it for him?" There's almost always a hidden motive that you don't know about. In the joint, nothing is free.*

- *Everything comes with a hefty interest rate. In time, your instincts will teach you whom to trust, if anyone. If someone offers you an apple, let's say, don't accept. You don't want to be taken to the prom in the middle of the night; if you get my drift.*

- *Find out how the inmate community works. Many inmates have been locked up before and will be able to give you information about how the internal system works, but you will have to judge for yourself whether to believe the information given. Use common sense and try to figure out if that person has a reason to lie or mislead you.*

- *Always be polite and respectful to guards and other prison officials, even if they present themselves as evil bastards. They hold all the cards, so never piss them off. Sure, some prison employees are better than others. But even so, never forget whose side they're on...it certainly isn't yours. Never challenge or debate anyone in power. You are never going to win.*

- *Never stare at anyone; inmates or guards. Understandably, you're new at this jail thing and may be curious about your new community members, but be careful. The inmate you may be staring at can completely misinterpret what you are doing. In the joint, if someone stares at you it usually means he feels intense hostility or disapproval towards you. Alternatively, staring is also a way of showing sexual interest. It's OK to look at people, but don't stare at them. Learn this very important difference.*

- *Never show fear, anger, happiness or pain. Emotions are your worst enemy and can reveal your weaknesses. Both inmates and guards prey on weaknesses. If someone can figure out what makes you angry, he can use that knowledge to manipulate you. Because people are around you 24/7, they have unlimited opportunities to test their manipulation skills on you.*

- *Don't join a prison gang. Prison gangs in the joint are more prevalent and more dangerous than on the outside. If you join a gang, you must obey all orders (criminal or immoral) given by the leaders, where the utmost loyalty is given. The other option is a severe beating, or worse, death.*

- *Respect other people's personal space and never allow others to invade yours. You will be tested, and if you allow others to get too close to you or your space, you will fall prey to everyone in the community. Personal possessions are very important to everyone who is locked up. Touching or using someone's personal possessions without permission will place you in physical danger.*

- *Watch your phone use. Big brother is listening at the other end and anything you say can and will be held against you. Never gossip about another inmate with your cellmate as it will get back to the other person. The joint is a very violent place. Watching what you say can save your life.*

- *Don't tell people anything they don't need to know. Choose your words carefully. Potentially, anything you say to guards or other inmates can be taken out of context and can be used to cause you harm. Some of the inmates you may encounter have short tempers; many are of low intelligence, and some are borderline mentally ill or just plain bad. Inmates like these don't come with a blinking warning sign attached to their foreheads. You can easily be misunderstood or deliberately misquoted by someone who's trying to set you up or start trouble.*

And that is life on the inside. Remember that the normal, rational rules of the outside world no longer apply. You will be living on a different planet with its own rules and codes of conduct. The only thing that should matter to you while in there is YOU and YOUR survival. Try to get through this experience with as little physical and mental damage as possible.

See you on the outs,

Dylan

UNTIL DEBT DO US PART

""It is our choices, Harry, that show what we truly are, far more than our abilities."

(J.K. Rowling)

Then there is the marriage piece that few experts talk about in addiction seminars and in those recycled, self-help books. There is a great human and financial cost among couples dealing with a loved one's addiction. Our son's addiction had almost bankrupted us mentally, emotionally, spiritually, and financially, and we not even recognizing the mess we were in. We became caught up in a cycle of accusing each other of being the weaker parent and the enabler of our son's behavior. It didn't matter who was right or wrong. Like loose sand, we felt the marriage begin to slip from under us from all the added pressures that came from our inability to deal with this problem as a united couple. We argued about the thousands of dollars we had spent on treatment costs and attorney fees; money that could have been better spent on family vacations, college, and our ruined trip to Italy. We walked around the house behaving like angry roommates. It had become easy to finger-point and snap at each other, making us feel doubly guilty. I know that in the heat of many moments, we made hurtful statements to each other that today we would both love to take back. The anguish became so unbearable that we even contemplated divorce, but truth be told who would want to take sole custody of a child in our son's condition.

I became consumed by this alien disease as I frantically tried anything to save my son; to stop his downward spiral. We tried to hide Dylan's problem from our other children and from our extended family, without much success. Friends and family members would look upon us with a strange curiosity.

Some would reach out with outpourings of compassion and consolation; others would openly accuse me of poor parenting or having enabling issues: *"You let him grow dredlocks? No wonder he's addicted."* And, *"You let him go to California, the drug mecca? No wonder he's f---ed up!"* And the one that still lies buried in my heart, *"You've ruined a perfectly happy, intelligent kid."* I was terrified beyond description.

I soon began to blame myself daily over things that I felt could have been different if I had only done things differently. My wife and I argued over the unhealthy obsession that just maybe, if we had been there more for our son or if we had thrown more *love* at the problem; if I would have been stricter then maybe something would have changed in him and trigger a willingness to seek help. We tried everything over and over again, and then we would retreat into the safety of our bedroom, and verbally flagellate ourselves when we didn't get the desired results. Woulda, coulda, shoulda. You could say that we were *shoulding* all over ourselves to no end.

Some people may argue that without pain there is no learning. And those 3C's quotes from Al-Anon were more of an annoyance than help: You Didn't **Cause** it; you can't **Control** it; and you can't **Cure** it kept ringing in my head. During our dark moments, I just couldn't buy it. Platitudes like these are best reserved for extraordinary souls like Nelson Mandela, Billy Graham or Mother Theresa, and I'm not one of them. In my dark moments, how could I have internalized such stuff? For ordinary guys like me, too much pain and suffering only makes us behave like gored bulls; out of control, and making us even more miserable.

Experts say that addiction is a family disease. At first, I didn't understand what that meant. I thought that Dylan was the one with the problem and the one who needed help. But in time I began to see how his sickness mirrored ours.

He was in a state of denial and so were we. He was suffering and we were suffering. He was out of control and we couldn't function properly. Our nerves were raw at how our son's addiction was not only ruining his own life, but ours as well. But we never gave up even during our darkest moments. We had to hold to the memory of the happy kid we knew Dylan to be. We were determined that somehow or another, things would turn out all right. We spent the next two years going from therapist to counselor, to Al-Anon groups and outpatient programs, none of which seemed to work. Many a night we would just fall into bed, exhausted and cry ourselves to sleep.

PRISON PARENTS

"Carry on my wayward son, there'll be peace when you are done."
(Kansas)

Our name is called over a crackling loudspeaker and we approach the front desk where an officer is finishing off a bag of Corn Nuts. Chewing dispassionately, he looks at our driver's licenses, then at our faces, and with a look of indifference, enters our names into a log book. We then sign another sheet of paper and are handed a pass with a number D-12 scrawled on it stating the module and the glassed cubicle where our son would be waiting for our visit. As I sign the form, I make eye contact with the officer without flinching as I hold myself back, afraid of the words that could spill out of my mouth. *"Asshole,"* I think. *"No one should be that important."*

We walk down a narrow, winding path with colorful flowers on each side that takes us deeper into the bowels of the county jail that ultimately leads to Module "D." The warmth of the sun and the beauty of the flowers do little to remove the hollow pain we now carry in the pit of our stomachs. We are more anxious to see how our son is doing and where God will lead his life next. Looking around the musty corridor, I am convinced that, just maybe, he is right where God needs him to be at this moment in his life. At least for now he's eating well and we don't have to worry anymore as to where he is every night. I sadly grin at my cynical sense of humor, and at suddenly realizing how quickly I have re-discovered my Higher Power.

We don't want to waste one minute of our half hour visit with our son, so we shuffle along looking for cubicle twelve. With my eyes fixed on the numbers on the glass panes, I hear my wife's muted cry, *"There's my boy!"*

We both struggle for space on this little round metal seat as we leap at the single brown telephone on the wall. There is a very thick glass window separating our visit, making it impossible to hear each other as the telephone has not yet been turned on. All the three of us can do is wait and look through the thick glass into each other's watery eyes. His baggy orange jumpsuit and his dingy, whitish-gray, faded t-shirt hang like a tarp over his tall, thin frame right down to his oversized, county-issued tennis shoes. Seconds later, *CLICK.* The telephone is on and our visit has begun.

In our joyful excitement, we all talk at once about anything and everything and nothing makes sense. Some of what we say is very upbeat and some of our words bring us to an awkward silence, then tears. But we all seem to understand that tears seem very appropriate right now, so we just let them flow. We continue to talk as time is precious. This is not the time to be hashing over all the reasons why our son is in there and the poor choices that got him where he is. We seem to have made a silent pact to save that conversation for another, more appropriate time. Today is just about talking, showing support, gathering strength and focusing on the future. We keep constantly changing topics so as not to shed too much light on the real questions. The bulk of the time is spent on talking about family stuff and we keep giving him encouragement to focus on the light at the end of the tunnel. We begin to get lively as we relax a bit and wallow in his warm smile and great sense of humor. He finds the courage to look at us with watery eyes to say, *"I'm really sorry about everything."* All we can do is nod and look at each other in silence. We don't know what to say.

Then suddenly, *CLICK*. Our thirty minutes are up and the telephone shuts off in the middle of our conversation. The feeling I get from that sound of closure is as close as I can imagine how an instantaneous heart attack might feel.

I sadly smile at him as we get up to leave. His mother blows kisses as his eyes cry out, *"Mom, don't let me go back in there!"* I know she wants to snatch him off his feet and take him away from that place. But she has to settle with placing her hand on the glass just like they do in the movies, even though we have been warned that it is not allowed. As for me, I just stand there dry-mouthed. I then pound my heart twice with my fist as I force a smile and point to him as I mouth the words, *"I love you, son."* As a guard leads him away, we watch with fixed eyes at his every move and just as we had hoped, he reaches the door that leads to what presumably is his cell block, turns to us and mouths back the words, *"I love you."*

The walk back to the car is mind-numbing. We quietly hold hands as our hearts continue to break. Through my wife's hand I feel not fear or sorrow, but instead a silent rage. I feel a mother's anger and unconditional love in her grip. A feeling that can only be expressed through the fury of a mother lion that has suddenly been separated from her cub, a kind of love no one but a mother can give.

This has been our first of many visits. As we drive away, I get this sinking feeling a parent gets when he is reminded that a family member has been left behind and that we need to turn around and bring him home, but we can't. The harsh reality is that now, we are *prison parents*. We did not choose this road, but we're walking it just the same.

USING IS A CHOICE
"Drug use is a choice; addiction is not."
(Al-Anon)

The first response that comes to mind when parents discover that their child suffers from an addiction is, *"Oh no, not our child! What did we do to cause this?"* Do you really think you were the cause of your teen's addiction? As parents we are often guilty of thinking that every negative issue our kids face is somehow our fault. But how can that be? We all have done our best as parents to provide a loving home environment, a good education, and the financial means for our children to live well and enjoy life. If you are a parent of a child suffering from drug addiction, the first thing you must accept is that it is not your fault. Our kids grow and change and are capable of making choices on their own. It's foolish to take the rap for what your teen has chosen to do. You are no more the cause of your teen's addiction than you are the cause for any of his successes. But if it makes you feel better, guilt and enabling are often inseparable and reside in a package called *parent*. If you happen to be one of the thousands of parents whose lives have been seriously put on hold by alcohol or drugs and are fighting the battle of your life, read on.

Living with an addicted loved one is not easy. It's downright challenging, exasperating, depressing and, yes, life-changing. Hopefully, by reading of our struggles you too will come to the same conclusion we did: regardless of your socio-economic status, the many titles you have earned, the degrees initialed at the end of your name, your safe neighborhood, good income, and whatever else you think will protect you, guarantees nothing. None of us are exempt from this cunning, baffling, and powerful disease; and we aren't all bad parents. Our teens are not *bad* or morally deficient either. It's just what they have become as a result of the poor choices they have made.

Addiction is a complex medical, genetic, psychological and social problem with multiple reasons behind it; a discussion best left to greater experts in the field. I only wish to point out to parents that whatever has transpired in your child's life thus far has had very little to do with outside, medical, psycho-social elements. Though they are real in that some people may be predisposed to addictions, but for the majority of young people in this nation, using alcohol and drugs is a choice, but unfortunately addiction is not. And until something healthier and more positive comes along, they will continue to seek out drugs and alcohol as their default coping mechanism and our addicted youth will continue to enter that proverbial revolving door called *treatment*.

MARIJUANA ADDICTION: Fact or Fiction?

"I get high with a little help from my friends."
(*The Beatles*)

Is marijuana addictive? For years this has been a common question and one of the most hotly contested drug debates to date. The short answer is that for most people, no, it is not addictive. Studies show that the majority of pot smokers don't become addicted. But for some people, kids especially, it can be addictive.   When dealing with the increased drug abuse incidents among young people today, just because addiction rarely happens doesn't mean it should be ignored. The *National Institute on Drug Abuse (NIDA)* recently reported that because of the potency of today's marijuana, more and more young people are beginning to show definite signs of marijuana dependency and are winding up at drug rehab clinics seeking treatment.

First-time users of pot are now younger. The drug itself has become stronger, and there is a greater variety of synthetic marijuana that can be purchased over the Internet or in music stores and it can easily be made available by kids at any bus stop near your home. There is no drug dealer per se. Today, our kids have become each other's dealers.

According to *NIDA*, marijuana remains the most commonly abused drug among teenagers today. More and more studies are showing that marijuana is clearly addictive in terms of psychological and social aspects. The traditional wisdom being marketed to young people by marijuana advocacy groups (*Americans for Safe Access,* and others) is that marijuana is an "earth-grown" herb and is not really as physically addictive as other manufactured drugs. They believe that marijuana use has now become a normal activity for most people and not harmful, and therefore nothing to worry about. They quote government studies that point to only five to ten percent of the marijuana using population meeting the classic criteria for addiction or dependency. These studies should not be considered noteworthy by any parent. Marijuana advocacy groups are categorically wrong, and here are the facts.

In numerous studies, long-term marijuana users have reported poor outcomes on a variety of life satisfaction and achievement measures, including educational attainment (*Texas State University study; National Institute on Drug Abuse, 2010*). With teens, marijuana use has psychological and social consequences that get in the way of their ability to perform well in school and make progress toward expanding their life goals. Neurological experts call this phenomenon *motivational syndrome*, a term that describes how high-inducing THC in pot inhibits or blocks receptors in the frontal cortex of the brain, and because a young person's brain is still in the development stages, the pot smoker will immediately begin showing signs of drained motivation, poor decision-making and other functional deficits. So, the mere fact that five to ten percent of the population becomes dependent on or addicted to marijuana, should be scary enough and worthy of national attention.

I'm not going to spray you with a lot of neurological or physiological jargon here (*cortex, neurotransmitters, synapses, dopamine,* etc), but please consider the following points about marijuana and apply them to dependence and addiction among young people:

Addiction-Dependency (Tomato-Tomahto)

Does dependency on marijuana mean that a person is addicted? Not in the general medical, treatment sense. But when it comes to chronic marijuana use, dependency and addiction can be considered the same. In practical terms, if a young person is using and wants to change his life, but can't because the dependency on the drug is too strong, then the fine line between dependency and addiction should not be a topic of debate. In treating adolescents for substance use, they are both the same.

I'm not going to spray you with a lot of neurological or physiological jargon here (*cortex, neurotransmitters, synapses, dopamine,* etc), just consider the following points about marijuana and apply them to dependence and addiction among young people:

1. There is evidence that marijuana activates reward centers in the brain which can impact a young person's self-control and motivation in negative ways.

2. There is evidence that marijuana stunts mental development in young people.

3. Habitual users seem to develop a tolerance in that it takes more of the drug to reach the same level of "high."

4. Marijuana users experience withdraw issues that are mild at first, but with habitual use people have reported cravings while others have expressed feeling *down* sluggish and unmotivated if they go without it. Most cannabis users do not recognize their behaviors as symptoms of withdrawals...such as irritability, difficulty sleeping (without the use), anger outburst and difficulty remembering.

5. Habitual users seem to feel irritable or agitated when not using.

6. There is evidence that alcohol and marijuana are indeed gateway drugs, and can lead young users to other substances which cause greater harm.

7. Persons dependent on marijuana continue its use even when negative consequences are mounting around them.

(Source: American Council for Drug Education, 2011)

These seven points seem to reinforce the idea that marijuana is not an innocent substance and arguably can be psychologically addictive.

Habitual users may not be physically hooked on marijuana, but they are highly dependent on it as a coping mechanism in their life. When taken, it can instantly transform a person's mood. One can be feeling sad, discouraged, upset, angry, or happy, but these feelings can easily be erased, masked or enhanced by smoking marijuana. It offers temporary relief and can get you so high, so quickly, that any emotional issues you might have been dealing with have been temporarily forgotten. With young people who are still in the developmental stages of life and learning to problem-solve, marijuana use and abuse can have severe implications.

A LOSS OF FREEDOM

Marijuana dependence can also be translated as a loss of freedom. Regardless of whether or not you buy into the idea that marijuana can be addictive physically, socially, or psychologically, being caught up in the daily lifestyle of smoking pot is still going to ultimately mean the same thing: loss of freedom. What more is addiction, really, than when your teen has to do something important, but is nervous and so he smokes a joint in order to normalize himself or when he has suddenly gotten into the habit of forgetting important details or appointments? And what do you call it when most of your teen's precious time is spent trying to find more pot in order to remain stable, but can't? So he then visits the local record shop to buy the synthetic stuff until he can replenish his real supply of pot. And, if your teen or loved one is put in jail for a drug-related crime then it's a no-brainer. He has *really* lost his freedom. If this is the case with your teen, then it matters little if we label it as addiction or dependency.

The fact of the matter is that, as a habitual user, your teen has become trapped in a cycle of drug use in order to feel normal enough to deal with the challenges of everyday life. That is addiction in anyone's book.

DEBATES DON'T MATTER

Is marijuana addictive? The argument is irrelevant. Marijuana dependency can easily dominate a young person's life and remove his or her freedom of choice, plain and simple. Just because it is considered a "soft" drug by proponents of its use, and does not have the extreme physical withdrawal symptoms, does not make it harmless. But, if you take a hard look at any young, heavy marijuana user who is battling the negative consequences of his dependency, you will see an addict nonetheless, and a life ruined by addiction. But instead of helping the user, we make jokes about him at comedy clubs, laugh at this human train wreck, and then judge him for the humiliating behavior that his addiction has caused. Like any disease, addiction is no laughing matter.

HOW DO YOU KNOW YOUR TEEN IS USING DRUGS?

"The road to disappointment is paved with expectations"
(Anonymous)

Does your teen shut down his laptop the minute you enter his room? Does he take all his phone calls outside? Has he begun to lose interest in school or his job? Has he given up his favorite hobbies to sleep all day? When you ask him what's up, do you get an evasive answer or tells you to mind your own business? When this happens, do you shut the door and quietly walk away. Folks, denial is more than a river in Africa.

You suspect drugs, right? But how can you tell for sure? There are general things to look for that are universal to all abusers, regardless of which drug they are using, and then there are specific symptoms of certain kinds of drugs. By learning the early signs of a loved one's drug and alcohol use, you may be able to avoid jail visitations like ours.

One often doesn't know if their loved one is using alcohol or drugs, but there are some early signs that I'm certain every parent of an addicted child has seen. First there is a sudden change in friendships where suddenly long-held relationships are replaced by sketchy characters you've never seen in your life. My mother used to say, *"When you lay down with dogs, you rise up with fleas."* This all makes sense. Young addicts both attract and feel attracted to other addicts. We're all human and prefer to associate with others who share our values, beliefs and lifestyles. That's perfectly normal. So why is it suddenly strange seeing our substance using kids suddenly building routine activities around people and places that attract and support their alcohol and drug use?

Persons working in the addiction field refer to this phenomenon as an *addicted-centered culture*: A network of people who have now disconnected from the normal socially-conforming lifestyle and have entered the addictive lifestyle of people who value the same things they do: drugs. Because of their sudden immersion in an addictive lifestyle, kids begin to experience the loss of important people in their lives and the lifestyle activities that was once the norm. I recall the hockey moms and dads whose kids carpooled with our son to tournaments and whose exchanges with us went from bright eyed smiles and hugs to distant hand waves. Those were the kind and sensitive ones. Others just plain shunned us. I'm talking serious shunning. The kind of shunning where you wave and they pretend they don't see you; a Bruce Willis in the *Sixth Sense* kind of shunning. Painful as it was we understood it, but they were doing it to our son and that's what hurt the most.

Then, there is a change in style of clothing or hairstyle. I recall as a young teen my mother saying each time I went out dressed in the seventies attire of the times, *"You are who you look like."* I wasn't a hippie; I just wanted to fit in *(sounds familiar?).* If your teen is suddenly walking around looking unkept and draped in bizarre clothing, then maybe it's time to investigate: This is only to say that any sudden changes overnight from what is socially "normal" to radical should be questioned. For example, if your child prefers to lock himself all day in his bedroom that reeks of incense and which has just been painted black with florescent figures, you better check it out. If in his bedroom he repeatedly listens to what today's kids call *slacker* music, he just may be what is referred today as a *loner stoner.* A shaved head, dreadlocks, a tie-dyed shirt or a Central American vest-poncho (known by users as "drug-rug") may not always turn someone into a druggie, but you can't argue that clothing and hairstyle announce loud and clear who you are long before you open your mouth.

Investigate it just to be safe. If you take the initiative to check things out in your own home and take your head out of the sand (denial), then it's a no brainer: *"If you look like a duck, quack like a duck, and walk like a duck, you must be a duck."*

Your suspicions may increase by noticing the inexplicable changes in school progress as your loved one's grades begin to take a dive. Looking back, I can tell you the semester, almost to the week, when our son started using just by his grades and attendance. You then discover that the school chums he has had since kindergarten have suddenly abandoned him. Nobody wants to be around a stoner. You begin to notice that he sleeps all day and is missing all night or is gone all weekend only to return home Sunday night, unkept and exhausted. With the progression of the disease, you begin to notice your loved one beginning to have difficulty handling personal and social responsibilities and law enforcement issues begin to increase, helloooo!

Finally, there is the change in ethics and values. He begins to lie, steal, and drop his enthusiasm for sports and hobbies. He loses stuff, and is always broke. These characteristics by themselves may not represent any real concern; however the more you add to your list the more it should trigger some curiosity on the part of any parent. Don't bury your head in the sand thinking that *this* cannot ever happen in your educated, middle class family or that with a little patience, he'll just grow out of it. That's denial at its best. Also, do not take signs of cheating on exams, manipulating the system and lying as rebellion or bad behavior where your only response becomes one of stricter rules and punishment. You did not teach him to be that way; he's that way because of his addictive lifestyle.

Ten Clues of Addictive Behaviors

Abuse of or addiction to alcohol or other substances is not always easy to spot. If many of the following clues are present, it could be that you are dealing with someone who needs help.

1. **Minimizing-** "I can stop anytime I want." Family minimization: *"He'll grow out of it."*
2. **Belligerence and intimidation-** Sarcasm, snapping, and general mean-spiritedness usually leads to the family feeling as though they must "walk on eggshells" around the addicted person.
3. **Lying and promise-breaking.** Both trademarks of substance abuse or addiction.
4. **Recurring financial difficulties-** You may witness repeated money crises, a lot of borrowing and a general sense that the using person is "digging a hole."

5. **Mood swings-** usually stems directly from the contrast of being under the influence (happy, calm, outgoing) or not (irritable, angry, withdrawn).
6. **Lack of self-responsibility-** People who abuse substances tend to habitually blame others for the negative circumstances in which they find themselves.
7. **Sense of entitlement.-**A common attitude is, "I don't have to see my P.O.," (*as in, " The rules don't apply to me."*)
8. **Oblivious to negative effects-** No matter how far down abusing people get, they often do not seem to "get" how bad things are.
9. **Surrounded by enablers.** Someone abusing alcohol or drugs likes to be around people who will cover up, make excuses for, or "rescue" them.
10. **Thriving on turmoil.** While there may be lots of drama, goals are never reached and there is little to show for all the "excitement."

Addicts and Alcoholics Lie...About Everything

"You didn't make it all the way to the beach just to drown on the sand."
(Dr. V to his son)

There, I said it. Lying and addiction are inseparable first cousins traveling hand-in-hand on the road to self-destruction and ruin. Anyone who hopes to provide assistance to someone traversing that dark trail needs to realize that everything an alcohol or drug-using person says or does must be taken with a huge grain of salt.

Some of the best con artists are boozers and users, and why not? They are on a 24-hour mission to protect their addiction so they can continue using. To do this, they need the engagement of victims; family members usually. Teens who are dependent on drugs can put on academy award performances just to cover up and maintain their addiction. There is no one more persuasive and genuine-seeming than an addicted teen (*and no one more gullible than the parent willing to believe*). He knows that what he is doing goes counter your house rules and most likely against the law, but doesn't want to risk being kicked out or arrested (*that would mean sobriety by default*). Another reason for lying is that your teen does not want to be forced to change and risk losing his using friends and the readily available supply of drugs. So he covers up his messes with lies and each lie covers up another until he comes to believe that everything he is saying is true. Eventually, he builds an alternate world around him made up of lies and dishonesty.

With Dylan, our trust and respect deteriorated with every lie until we didn't know our teen anymore and we found ourselves disliking the liar he had become. So don't take it personally when your teen begins to lie about his addiction. It's all a part of keeping his illness alive.

When the lying starts, about how he's going to get help, get a job or go to college, and nothing happens, call him on it without shaming, set some boundaries, and keep offering him outside help. Let him know his lying bothers you and until he gets help you aren't buying anything he says nor will you aide in his destructive path.

This kind of no-nonsense approach may not be the best solution in every circumstance, but you have an addict in your home. And when your addicted loved one lies, he is attempting to hide the truth about a deadly and destructive secret that must not be allowed to remain hidden in the shadows. Only when you consistently call him on it and set consistent boundaries, will he find the incentive to stop. And, if you can finally get him to reveal the truth about what has been happening in his life, the chances of ultimately getting help and defeating his drug or alcohol addiction will be tremendously enhanced.

ENABLING QUESTIONAIRE

Enabling refers to the process by which family members, such as partners and parents allow or *enable* an addicted person to continue in their addictive behaviors, by failing to recognize the problem, not setting appropriate boundaries and covering up the trail of messes your loved one has left behind.

Answer the following questions to determine if you're enabling your loved one's behaviors.

1. Yes   No   Have you ever 'called in sick' for your loved one?

2. Yes   No   Have you ever made excuses for your loved one's behavior?

3. Yes   No   Have you ever lied to anyone about your loved one's behavior?

4. Yes   No   Have you ever bailed your loved one out of jail?

5. Yes   No   Have you ever paid for his or her legal fees?

6. Yes   No   Have you ever paid bills your loved one's bills?

7. Yes   No   Have you ever 'loaned' your addicted loved one money?

8. Yes   No   Have you ever given your addicted loved one chance after another?

9. Yes   No   Have you ever finished jobs that your loved one failed to complete?

10. Yes   No   Have your secrets comprised your
    relationships with your spouse?

11. Yes   No   Have you often considered just walking
    out on your family?

List five more things you have done that could be considered
enabling behaviors.

1._____

2._____

3._____

4._____

5._____

What it means: *The more items you check, the more likely it is that you may be enabling (aiding) your addicted loved one in avoiding the consequences of his or her own actions.*
 (Source: Al-Anon)

LETTER TO MY SON: Week Four

Good morning son:

"It is what it is." This street Zen saying couldn't be truer as I begin to adjust to our situation. I couldn't sleep this morning so I went for a short, brisk walk to the park half a mile away. I ran half-way back just for the exercise and I am now sipping a (lukewarm) cup of coffee and staring at these obscure fonts on the computer. Today will be humid and 85 degrees. The sky has a dirty, gray hue about it and there is barely a breeze blowing the leaves on the trees. It is a typical summer around here and the squash and tomatoes that I planted last spring are drowning in their own summer sweat. I'm in a bad mood today as you can tell. I'm still brooding over what has happened to you and where you have now been placed. But let me wallow in this mood for a little while longer, before I have to put on my game face and get back into the fray.

I received your latest letter and have noticed that each one gets longer. That is a good thing. They seem filled with your thoughts of how you're going to get through it all. I'll try to respond to those thoughts as I write each week. My notes to you may seem random as writing about personal issues and feelings seem somewhat alien to me. This not writing like when you were away at hockey camp. Writing has become different now; more intense, more personal. I don't always like to put my head on paper. It's too revealing and exposes some *thing* in me that I haven't yet come to understand.

I have always been good at dodging sensitive topics, but this time there is no escape route. It's just you and me, inside each other's head. Writing will now become great medicine for both of our minds and souls. I read somewhere that there is no greater friend than a blank sheet of paper. So keep writing, son. Keep asking. And I will respond as honestly and frankly as I can. So let's begin.

I hope that by now you have learned that guards don't play in there. They don't care how young you are; they will still lock you up like an animal. Now, I'm sure you are spending these days going over in your head just how you are going to adjust to this new change. I can only imagine how spirit-crushing these recent weeks have been on your body, mind, and soul. You have now been moved to a section you were hoping to avoid all along; no sunshine, no freedom to move about, and not knowing how you're going to be able to hold it together as you face the balance of your time in that 8x10 cell with an accused murderer for a *cellie* (jail term for cellmate). You know that your safety has always been our primary concern and not being able to protect you frightens the hell out of us. Hopefully our letters, cards and the books that are now trickling in from family and friends will be of great help to you. I understand that everyone has sent all that you have requested. Just know that we are still here to support you in any way we can. We will never abandon you.

I wince each time I press the rewind button in my mind and revisit the time this whole thing began. How did we get to this point? Instead of anger, my strongest response throughout all this has been a feeling of profound guilt; guilt at my going against the family's opinion and letting you go to California, a mecca for drugs, free lifestyles, and totally unsupervised. Couple this with my selfish desire to have you get out of the Midwest and experience life on your own as I once had. It comes as no surprise that you wound up where you are today.

Lately, I have become more and more obsessed with that same profound guilt. A feeling that perhaps, through a selfish desire to live my life through you, I may have set you up.

Say nothing of the thundering roar coming from the crowd in my recurring nightmares, "*See, we told you so. We knew he wasn't ready!*" I have been struggling with these and other emotions for several weeks. Outside of writing, private talks with your mom, and a little prayer from time to time, there has been no one outside this circle with whom to share my feelings.

I'd be lying if I said this tumultuous journey you're on hasn't affected me. It has – BIG TIME! But just like you, I have also begun to cope through it all and am finally learning how to say *enough-of-this* and begin to mean it. There comes a time in our lives when we finally get it; when the voice in our head cries out, "Enough!" Pretty crazy, right? I've slowly begun to process and work through this, and I'm coming to the realization that, just maybe, this was nobody's fault, and for sure, not mine. Outside of needing to set stronger boundaries; be a little more forceful with you, something inside says that you still would have used.

I can now clearly say to myself that I didn't cause this to happen and so I won't take ownership for your actions, son. I have slowly begun to accept the fact that perhaps you just might have made the same selfish, unthinkable choices where else you might have gone off to. I don't know. I can only deal with the present and it shows me that you set the wrong priorities for yourself even before you left the Midwest. I hope you too have had enough; that jail has been your *hitting bottom*. Let's talk more about this when I fly down to visit with you.

Until we fish again, stay at peace where you are at.

Love, Dad.

WHEN HELPING DOESN'T HELP

"He's tried to make me go to rehab; I won't go, go, go."
(Amy Winehouse)

No one wants to believe that their teen has a problem with alcohol or drug use. Too often we let our good judgment become blinded by denial. We even go so far as to claim ownership of our kid's problems and talk ourselves into believing that the fault is all ours. We love them so much that we are willing to do anything just to protect them; to remove any pain they may be suffering. If your child is standing in the middle of the railroad tracks and a train is coming full steam, wouldn't you push him away even at the risk of your own life? What good are fathers if not for these things?

Addiction became our new reality. It quickly broke down all communication and separated what was once a tight knit family. We began to take sides instead of uniting in helping our loved one. We avoided many social functions and often isolated ourselves for fear of shame and embarrassment at having an addict in our family. Family fun had become a distant memory.

Take it from someone who's been there and has the T-shirt to prove it. Sometimes helping just doesn't help. Enabling our son and lying to ourselves only prolonged our pain and possibly his addiction. The real tragedy was that the more we helped our son, the more he became crippled and the more we unknowingly slowed his recovery. What we didn't know was that the longer it takes for parents to decide to stop rescuing, the further the disease advances. Many people think the disease only lies with the individual suffering from it, but experts in the field of addiction have shown over and over again that addiction is a family disease.

Families need to understand the insidious nature of addiction and how a perfectly healthy family can be caught in the middle of a losing battle if they don't prepare themselves with the proper information, tools, and support.

It's a harsh reality, but it took us several years of failure to begin to get it; that maybe this was not our fault; that just maybe Dylan loved the drugs more than any consequence of even going to jail just to get more of it. Soul searching can sometimes provide a family with some pretty harsh truths! But this doesn't have to become your journey. You cannot throw everything at a metaphorical wall called *addiction* and expect your teen to change. The truth is he won't! We tried it. That wall is more powerful than all of us.

Fifteen Rounds with Tyson

No doubt, you are probably living our same nightmare. At first, I tried repeating Al-Anon's Three *C's* quotation, but it just wouldn't sink in. I have since learned that by feeling responsible for my son's addiction I had unknowingly believed that my influence on him was so powerful that just maybe I might have influenced his addiction as well. I thought that if I had just done things a little differently, if I had done it *right,* then maybe I could have controlled it, and perhaps even cure it and have everything come out the way I wanted. I came to believe that my love for my son was stronger than any addiction. I did not realize that these arrogant feelings of superiority were really feelings of inferiority based on fear; a defensive reaction I had incorporated against this new, strange and nagging feeling of helplessness at seeing my son slip away from our protective grasp. His addiction had become my equal, and it soon overpowered me. It was as if I was going fifteen rounds with Mike Tyson. You could say that I was rendered helpless and the addiction that had taken over our son's spirit seemed to just laugh in my face.

I found myself reacting and jabbing at shadows like a tired boxer I had become, crouched in a corner and never connecting a punch. It was quite a rude awakening to being outsmarted and beaten by some *thing* I could not put my hands around. I became so exhausted that at times I just wanted to crawl into a small space and sleep. A coma would've been nice; or amnesia.

NOT EVERY GREAT MAN IS WISE

"If drugs kills millions o brain cells, why haven't they killed the one's that make me want to use?"

(Mario, high school student in recovery)

Having a loved one in jail or prison can be very stressful and dispiriting. It's now our son's eighth week in lock-up and I get to see him for three days as it is a holiday weekend. My wife and I travel separately now, and on alternate months as flying together has been very tight on our budget. We have begun paying most of our living and travel expenses with our Travel VISA where free air miles are logged. We don't rent a car anymore. Instead we catch a shuttle to the hotel closest to the county jail. We then walk or use Rapid Transit. My wife, the classy lady, stays at the Double Tree in the mall just across from the jail, and on the third floor where she can easily see the jail complex below, perhaps hoping to get a glimpse of her son. I've heard of people dealing with pain in different ways, but what she is doing to herself is just plain torture. Unfortunately for me, I stay at is in a Motel Six in a sketchy part of town where the gangs are thicker than cockroaches, and where the streets are named after famous persons like Martin Luther King Blvd., JFK parkway, and Cesar Chavez Ave. and Lincoln Highway. Why, I wonder, do civic leaders place the names of the most peaceful people in history in the most violent parts of their cities? The *SIX* as the motel is referred to by the gangs fits my budget and it's only six blocks from the facility.

Early Sunday mornings bring different people to this place. This is clearly a different set of folks from the gang-bangers who line up on Fridays and Saturdays. This group seems more mature and most have a look of quiet defeat. Over where the line makes a turn closest to the entry stands a taller man. He is lanky and seems somewhat pale.

His eyes are sunken and his skin is wrapped tightly around his face. Protruding from his weathered Levi jacket are his hands, calloused by the hard work and hard times he has endured. A roofer or a gardener I presume. And there are others one could write a book about. These are the wives and families of someone they love very much and for whom they have foregone their only day off from work just to be here.

As the line moves up, I keep going back to a recurring thought in my head, "I'm one of them." That is, I share a kinship with everyone here. My heart breaks for them. A great philosopher (Cervantes, Aquinas, Bertrand, it's not important) once said that *suffering builds character*. This morning, I just don't buy it. Not every great man is wise. What the people in this line know firsthand, and philosophers know little about is that suffering also destroys people, both spiritually and psychically. It stings to be here, but it is what it is. For some of us in this line, life has become an incredibly difficult and painful journey.

Once in, and an hour later, my son's name is called and I will once again walk through the glass door that leads to the building where my son is housed. I have now been acquainted with the long winding path and its manicured flowers, bougainvilleas, and Hawaiian ferns that lead to my son. The array of colors and the bright sunshine mean nothing to me as the anger and guilt I have built up over the months has sucked the colors of life from everything.

As I enter the wing where my son now resides, I once again review in my mind those words of encouragement I wrote and practiced on the plane. I anxiously look for booths *one* and *nine*. You're not going to believe this, but booths one and nine have significant meaning to the jail staff. Booth one is for Mexican/Hispanic inmates and nine is for African Americans.

The rest are for white and others. The jail staff feels that segregation reduces racial tension between these groups. Let's see, how this came about. A team of highly paid social scientist conducted an extensive breakthrough study of inmate behaviors in the penal system and devised a scientific model which could guarantee positive race relations in America's jails and prisons and they called it *racial segregation*. Now that's what I call social progress.

I spot booth number one and make a nervous dash for it. On the other side, my son enters and his smile lights up the place. His hair has been buzzed Marine-style and his glasses have been repaired with white medical tape. I nervously scan his body looking for scars or missing parts. He looks me over as well with a, *"Hey, Dad. Good to see you."* He looks just like any normal teenager in an orange costume, only behind a four-inch glass separation. It takes us a minute to take each other in as I lay all my anger aside, and admit to him that it feels good to see him again. He expresses gratitude for my taking the time to fly all the way to see him.

I notice he's sporting a fresh pair of orange overalls that still drape over him like a tarp. As the phone is activated I repeat to myself what my wife instructed me to do: stay strong, don't scold or lecture, and stay calm. Scanning him for cuts and bruises has now been a common part of my visits as we go through our awkward opening dialogue: *"How's mom doing?"* *"She's Fine, she says hello."* *"How's the job?"* *"You know, same-old-same-old."* And so on. *"Dad, Check this out,"* he says as he places a foot on the counter to show off his new set of county-issued, orange tennis shoes and a clean pair of brightly colored socks. *"I get to pick my own clothes now that I work in the laundry."* His display of joy brings us both to laughter which at first is quiet and restrained.

Then suddenly, right there in front of the whole visiting area, laughter just simply starts pouring out of both of us. I discover this deep swell of momentary joy coming from the pit of my stomach. I had not laughed from down there in a long time. I just wanted to grab and hold him like I used to when he was a kid. I have never felt more clean and alive since, well, I don't remember when.

Eventually we both calm down and begin muddling through current events, the will Obama be elected, how the Lakers are doing, and how he plays a lot of card games (*Spades* being the new favorite) and how he must look and act older than he is. Finally we both run out of time and things to talk about. Our silence signals that he must now get down to the core of what we are both waiting for. Running his hands nervously through his buzz cut, he blurts out what he has been postponing so long. *"Dad, I've had a lot of time to look back at everything now,"* he says. *"I'm really sorry for all the problems I've caused the family. With all the time I now have, all I do is lay in my bunk and think about how I might have ruined things for everyone. I really had it made, but I now see how badly I messed things up."*

All I can do is stare at his clean-cut features as I try to keep my composure. I fidget nervously as I try to find the words I have been practicing on the plane. My mind feels like the overstuffed carry-on bag back at the hotel. With my mouth dry and my voice cracking, the words I had been practicing begin to spill from my mouth all at once, *"No son. You haven't messed up your life. This is merely a setback, and while you may be facing some serious jail time, we are a tight family and you will always be our son. I know that for your own good you need to be strong and act like you are older than your age, but no matter how old you are or where you live, you will always be our son and we will never give up on you. You got that?"*

CLICK! The phone has been de-activated. As he opens the door that presumably leads him back to his cell block, Dylan mouths the words, *"See you tomorrow."* I had forgotten that Monday was a holiday and had one more visitation. Nevertheless, I feel that each visit seems like the last.

Visiting my son was both a terrible and wonderful experience. Regardless of what anyone thinks, I believe that for now, this place is the best place for him to think through his brief detour in life. At least we know he is alive, he is clean, and he is safe. He seems to have become stronger now that he's sober, and he seems to be working through things the best way he knows how. Has he felt guilty about all he has done? I don't know, but that's not what we're after. Has he taken the first steps toward owning up to the mess he has created? I hope so unless he's conning himself. If he is, then it's too bad for him.

Monday afternoon, as the airport shuttle takes me along PCH (Pacific Coast Highway) to the airport, the rush of the ocean breeze clears my head, ushering a feeling of momentary relief and hope; relief that for the moment everything has turned out well, and hope that my son has a shot at a new life. Maybe I'm conning myself, but if his apology and our solid eye contact are any indicators, he seems to have taken a first, but important step. My hopes have become tentative, though. I'm not holding my breath.

THE TURNING POINT
"Nothing changes until something changes."
(Earnie Larsen)

During those dark days, after his release and his transfer back to the Midwest, Dylan's addiction escalated and began to cause us a lot pain that for a period had our lives turned upside down. Some of the dreams and expectations (*college, travel, and career*) I had for Dylan had all gone down the drain. I didn't know quite how to handle it. I ran around the house frantically trying to maintain stability in the family; feeling like a juggler or plate spinner in the circus, balancing my and our family's emotions at once. It's as if something in my life was out of order and there was nothing I could do to fix it. Some days I would spend time outside just moving furniture around the patio, then repeating the same routine the next day thinking that by keeping busy I could purge the pain and despair I held deep down in my gut. There was one time I recall cleaning my boat and crying without wanting to, and in a way that I had never cried before; not since I was a young boy. It scared me to be so angry, helpless, and out of control.

ADDICTED TO THE ADDICT

We became so steeped in shame, denial, and preoccupied with our son's drug problem that it was like we had become addicted to the addict. The realization jumped out at me like a giant neon sign, blinking brightly in my face: *enabler...enabler...enabler.* How could I, a professional in a helping profession, not connect the dots sooner? I had come to my moment of clarity and furious with myself at learning that I had become too close to the problemto see what was happening to our family.

I then revisited the research to confirm what I had already learned in graduate school and if there were any similarities in what I was doing and what experts in the field say about *enabling* and *codependency*. I learned that nothing had changed and that enablers were still people who, in their intent to help a dysfunctional person solve a problem, make the problem worse by trying to clean up the messes left behind, thus allowing the dysfunctional person to continue on their path of self-destruction.

Upon further review, I learned that codependency is still defined as someone having a compulsive need to control a person or an otherwise out of control situation in a way that is unhealthy for all concerned. What do you know, guilty as charged.

STOP IN THE NAME OF LOVE

"A very important part of being kind to ourselves is learning how to say no."
(Robert Burney)

Rescuing and cleaning up after someone who is actively practicing their addiction is not love; it's enabling; plain and simple. Helping your addicted loved one from time to time is understandable and important if he is visibly and verifiably taking steps toward recovery. That is being supportive in a positive manner. Helping him continue on his self-destructive path by lying and covering up is not supportive, and for sure doesn't fall under the definition of unconditional love.

To find out if you're an enabler or co-dependent, answer these eight simple questions:

1. Do you confuse being needed with being loved?

2. Do you loan money to your loved one, but never get it back nor do you ask for it?
3. Do you relate best with others by taking care of them?
4. Do you repress your anger just to maintain the peace?
5. Do you blame yourself for the negative actions of your loved one?
6. Do you feel guilty after helping or rescuing an addicted loved one?
7. Do you put yourself last in your family unit?
8. Do you say *yes* when you mean *no*, and *no* when you mean *yes*?
9. Do you set boundaries and then cave in?
10. Are your young adult children (above 18 years of age) unable to stand on their own two feet?

If you answered no to these questions, you can skip this chapter. But if any of your answers are yes, then let's talk.

I don't know if the above is where we were as parents, but it felt pretty darn close. I realized I was too close to the problem and couldn't disengage from it. Even as a human services professional, I never thought I would have codependency issues, until I became obsessed with trying to help my son solve *his* problems.

Enabling: Impediments to Recovery

Dolly Parton, the famous country singer was attributed with saying, *"It ain't easy being easy,"* and in the world of enabling and codependency she was right. It works something like this: The chemically dependent person is being shielded by the enabler from the negative consequences of his use. The purpose in life of a chemically dependent person is to continue using. The purpose in life of the enabler is to protect the user from consequences, but not knowing that he is simply facilitating the addict's continued use. The enabler typically tries to hold things together in the name of love, until the anger and frustration mounts. The enabler continues to walk on eggshells so as to not to anger the white elephant in the room, making wall-to-wall mistakes in the process of trying to help and cover up until he or she can no longer keep a lid on things. Where and how does the madness end? Below are some common mistakes made by parents exhibiting enabling behaviors:

Questions That Make You Go ...Hmmm!

1. Have you at any time lied to the attendance office at school or his probation officer? (Why, *so he could see that consequences don't apply to him, so he can continue getting high?*).

2. Have you bought him a car to commute to his job because it snows hard in winter? (*Not understanding that the addict in him would gladly walk miles in the deep snow, barefoot, just to get*

more drugs, but now he can drive to his drug hook-ups.)

3. Have you paid for his traffic tickets? (Why, *so he could show the world that he is unaccountable to society?).*

4. Have you loaned him gas money to get to his job or an AA meeting? (*Why, so he can save his paycheck to buy more drugs?).*

5. Have you bargained with him just to get him sober? (*Why, so that the addict in him could blow off his part of the agreement and lose his temper each time you protested?).*

6. Have you ever paid for his rent deposit? (*Why, so he could have his own drug den with your money? Woo hoo!)*

7. Have you ever done things for your loved one that he could do himself? (*Why, to make him feel helpless and send a message that he can't be successful without your involvement?)*

Things Enablers Say

- *"This the LAST time."*
- *"He's different. He's only a recreational user."*
- *"Leave him alone. He'll grow out of it."*
- *"It's only a teenage phase."*
- *"I'd rather he drank at home."*
- *"This time it's different. He's really going to quit. I can feel it."*
- *"If we hadn't gotten divorced, things would be different."*
- *"If he hadn't had such a bad family life, things would be different."*
- *"He's ADHD, what can I do?"*
- *"Get a lawyer. He has too much potential to be facing jail time."*

And the worse one:

- *"He needs me. He can't function without my help."*

How many more can you add?

1. _____
   _____

2. _____
   _____

3. _____
   _____

4. _____
   _____

5. _____
   _____

There are numerous other clues to determine whether one is an enabler, but it boils down to two words: *sympathetic* and *empathetic*. There is a world of difference between these two words. Sympathy can sometimes be misinterpreted for pity. Pity usually suggests a power imbalance between the person showing pity and the pitied, and a show of compassion or mercy.

Because addicts are highly manipulative thinkers, your display of sympathy can be misunderstood by the addict as being entitled to aid or at the very least giving him permission to continue along his destructive journey because you *feel* for his problem.

Empathy on the other hand, means having a compassionate understanding of someone's pain: *"I can understand how someone in your situation would feel that way, but I still don't condone what you are doing to yourself."* Empathy is showing your understanding of the problem and supporting your loved one in his struggle toward recovery without being pulled into the addictive process yourself. Empathetic people do not allow themselves to be used. Saying "No" is easy. It only has two words and you don't have to explain what you mean.

I think you get the picture. Do you still think you can have a normal, rational relationship with your addicted loved one? Forget it! Whatever relationship you had before he ingested whatever he has coursing through his body, has now terminated. Your job now is to stay focused on the solution and not the problem. It's okay to love your loved one, but do it in a way that *detaches* you (with love) from the problem and allows you to work on solutions that don't ensnarl you in his addictive drama.

IT AIN'T EASY BEING EASY: Signs of Codependent Behaviors

HOW DO YOU STAND WITH YOUR USING LOVED ONE? ARE YOU HELPING OR HINDERING?

1. Yes   No   Have you ever lost time from work due to helping your loved one.

2. Yes   No   Have your relationships suffered due to your loved one's addiction?

3. Yes   No   Have you set boundaries and then backed down (or out)?

4. Yes   No   Do you control financial situations that belong to your loved one?

5. Yes   No   Have you ever felt remorse after giving in to a situation?

6. Yes   No   Do you feel guilty playing the good guy/bad guy role with your addicted loved one?

7. Yes   No   Have you ever borrowed money to finance your addict's needs?

8. Yes   No   Do you feel guilty or reluctant to purchase things for yourself?

9. Yes   No   Has this problem caused you to take less care of yourself?

10. Yes   No   Have you ever dragged leftover pain into current discussions?

11. Yes   No   Does your addicted relationship caused you to lose sleep?

12. Yes   No   Do you find yourself blaming your or your spouse for this condition?

13. Yes   No   Have you accepted some blame for your
                 loved one's behavior?

14. Yes   No   Have you ever considered self-
                 destruction as a result of this?

What does this mean: Answering **"yes"** to any of these questions puts you at risk of being codependent. More than three positive responses may indicate that codependency may already be a problem in your life.

Children under the age of 18 don't have the option of refusing treatment. However, if your child is over the age of 18 they must voluntarily enroll in a treatment program or face the consequences of their addiction whatever those consequences may be.

It will become necessary for you to take a no nonsense approach and create boundaries that protect you, your family, and the addicted person. If you don't or cannot follow through, more than likely you will continue to live with an untreated addict until he or someone close to him is destroyed by it.

RECLAIM YOUR POWER

"It's a family affair; it's a family affair."
(Sly and the Family Stone)

There is a story I wish to share with you about a psychologist who was conducting a training session on stress management: *As he walked around the room, he held out a glass of water in his hand. As he raised the glass of water we all thought, "He's not going to do the "half-empty; half-full" schtick is he?" Instead, with a smile on his face he inquired, "How heavy is this glass of water?" Our answers ranged from 8oz. to 16oz. and everything in-between.*

He then replied, "The absolute weight of this glass doesn't matter. It depends on how long I hold it. As he outstretched the glass he continued, "If I hold it for ten minutes, it's not a big problem. If I hold it out here for an hour, I'll get an ache in my arm. If I hold it for a day, my arm will feel numb and paralyzed. In each case the weight of the glass doesn't change, but the longer I hold it, the heavier it becomes."

He then continued, "The stress and worries in life are like that glass of water. Think about your problems for a short while and nothing happens. Think about them a little longer and they begin to hurt. And if you think about them all day long and beyond, you will feel paralyzed and incapable of getting anything done. Always remember to put the glass down.

Dramatic changes are possible when families learn to put their problems (the glass) down momentarily and maintain a proper perspective when dealing with a loved one's substance abuse. Many young people who have recovered from addiction attributed much of their successful recovery to their parents' commonsense and strong, non-judgmental family support.

There will be many days and months of struggle. Although the journey is tough, it is possible to survive it, and enjoy life as a family once again. I want to repeat my earlier statement with conviction that your loved one isn't *crazy, immoral* or *bad* and that it's possible he can regain his life. But it's all comes down to how you react to the illness.

Knowing how to react will make all the difference in your loved one's life. Throughout this whole ordeal, four things have stood out in my mind more than anything else: 1) Knowledge is power. You must have accurate information if you are to help your loved one through his substance use disorder; 2) sometimes you need to step aside and let natural consequences take over; 3) you must set solid boundaries and stick to them; and 4) the family works as a unit in addressing the challenges of this dreadful disease. Family chaos and divorce are by-products of families not working together. Give yourselves a break, as the story I have just shared, put the glass down for a moment and focus on each other. Don't become a doormat for your addict. Instead, begin to reclaim your power, happiness, and life by working as allies.

The following action steps can place you on the right path:

ACTION STEPS

1. Be honest with yourself about your loved one's addiction. Educate yourself and learn the facts by obtaining reliable information from experts in the field or from local support groups that address addiction issues. The more you learn about addiction, the sooner you will understand your loved one's struggle with substances and be in a better position to help.

2. Realize this was not your fault. But you have learned that already.

3. Don't try to fix this problem on your own. Often parents who are blaming themselves for their loved one's addiction will, out of shame, try to fix the problem not knowing that addiction cannot be fixed. Sometimes we are too close to the problem and too emotional to see things objectively. Seek wise counsel immediately.

4. Practice detachment. Chaos, drama and addiction are all first cousins. Part of coping with an addicted loved one is insulating yourself from the problem. Because addicts are manipulative thinkers the addiction will swallow you up like quicksand along with your loved one.

5. Give yourself a break. Care for yourself first. You can't help other members of your family if you have been driven to poor mental and physical health by your loved one's addiction. Also, don't let other family members take a back seat to your loved one's addiction.

6. Take walks with your spouse. Give it a name: *walk and talk.* It worked for us and maybe it can work for you. If the anger persists, or if you are still feeling emotionally paralyzed, seek professional help.

7. Avoid playing the blame game with your spouse as this is counterproductive and harmful to the relationship/

8. Become an ally to your spouse. Take care of your relationship as it can easily be destroyed when a loved one becomes addicted. Don't fold up your tent and abandon your responsibilities to yourself and your spouse.

9. Avoid counter-productive analysis of the problem, events, or motives. Things are as they are. There may not be any underlying causes. Looking for answers to unanswerable questions can quickly get exhausting and unhealthy.

10. Stop the anger-pity teeter totter reaction to the problem. As parents, we first get angry at our addicted loved one, and then we make threats. We then preach, lecture, and make more angry threats. And when the anger subsides, we feel pity for the loved one. This is very painful for both the loved one and the family. An addicted person is not motivated to take positive action through pity, love, guilt, and intimidation.

11. Set boundaries and stand firm. Say what you mean and mean what you say; but never say it mean.

12. Never allow yourself to become codependent. You are a supporter, not an enabler. You can't allow your loved one to get away with manipulation: saying he can't do things when he can, and not taking responsibility for his own life. Let him use the same energy he used to find drugs to figuring things out on his own.

13. Get with your Creator. You will not find a situation greater than the one you're currently in where you will need a link to a Higher Power.

(**Sources:** *Beverly Conyers, Al-Anon, AA, Angelyn Miller*)

LETTER TO MY SON: Week Seven

"God, I've made a mess of things. Teach me the right way to be."
(OCC inmate's prayer)

Hello son:

How are you holding up in this rude awakening? I have received your letter and am deeply concerned about how you are constantly pacing and feeling that you're going to lose your mind in that cage you're in. Believe me, you won't. Your transfer to a different *mod* has been a tough adjustment and you are going to have peaks and valleys, but I'm certain that you'll make it through. Naturally you're feeling frustrated. I feel you. Change does that to a person. Feeling overwhelmed? I understand that, too. I can only imagine the pain of being locked up in a small mod with hardened criminals. Still, there is no ducking your situation, son. It is time to face the music and begin looking deep inside yourself by taking inventory of your gifts and talents, and how you want to use them once you get out. All this suffering must have a purpose.

This is the time to start by committing to something worthwhile. Use what is left of your time to keep your mind, body and spirit alive and healthy. As you rise each morning think to yourself, *"How can I help myself by helping others less fortunate, who never receive letters, books or calls from home?"* Maybe the books that friends and family have sent you can be shared with others, and serve as that spark that lights up someone else's day; someone like you, perhaps, who may also be attempting a shot at self-understanding and is feeling that he, too, is about to lose it.

Funny how I have found my Higher Power throughout this ordeal. It may be hard to believe, but God may have handpicked you from jail and is forging you like metal for greater things. He has a funny way of doing things. Just think of all the misfits God has chosen to do His work. There's Moses, an inarticulate, stuttering shepherd who challenged the Pharaoh and freed his people from bondage; and what about Paul the Apostle? Here's a guy who went around killing Christians all over the Roman Empire and yet was hand-picked by God to write two thirds of the bible's New Testament. Then there is Desmond Tutu, Sister Theresa and others too numerous to mention who may have been chosen by God for a specific purpose. So what's so strange about God hand-picking a scared, lanky kid out of jail to mold and get into shape for the task of helping others in greater need? God's not done with you yet, son. For now, continue keeping your walk-and-talk with God personal and simple.

I'm not the greatest religious role model, and what I'm about to reveal to you may shock you, but a lot of what I'm feeling about what God has done for our family lately is beginning to have an impact on the way I look at things. As I go through my days I sometimes pray for myself. I pray that I learn to understand, not just as a father, but perhaps as a future servant. I keep getting hints of His answer, and perhaps, in all this confusion, He's trying to tell us both something; that what we have been doing no longer works and that it's time for a new approach. Hang in there son, the answers will all become clearer soon.

Until we fish again, be at peace where you are at.

Love, Dad.

THE FEAR OF SETTING BOUNDARIES

"Enabling is not a selfless act. It is a selfish one and it is not love."
(Shannon, a student in recovery)

As you read about our journey, take a good look at yours and the sick nature of what we do as parents in the name of love. Do you really think you have been rescuing your teen out of concern or unconditional love? This is not a pleasant message to deliver, but it is one you need to hear. You really have been rescuing out of *FEAR* and not love. But before you put this book down and use it as a coaster, listen up. People do bizarre things for their addicted ones, not so much out of love, but out of fear of setting boundaries and the resulting consequences.

Parents often think that if they *tough-love* their child, they risk losing the relationship they have clung to so dearly. What relationship? Right now, your child's only loyalty is to his drug of choice, not to you. Then there is the fear that if you set strict standards or evict him from your home, you may lose him to the streets or that he may be injured or worse. I'm not one to recommend other peoples books, but if I have just described your journey and are dealing with some heavy guilt over it, do yourself a favor and read: *Healing the Wound* by Mathias Karayan MA., and *Dependent No More* by Melodie Beatie. Both books were helpful in healing and can be found on Amazon.com.

If what you have just read sounds familiar, then it probably is. Setting boundaries is one of the hardest things a parent can do, but it's one sure way of taking control of what is essentially a no-win situation. We found our greatest challenge in setting boundaries was identifying that thing we would not put up with, then sticking to it.

Another challenge and one which took a lot of practice was trying to set boundaries without emotional detachment. I, more than my wife, found myself doing it all wrong. I kept crying out like a madman, *"I only have three rules you must follow in this house; no lying, no stealing, and no drugs. What is so hard about that?!!"* My blood pressure was in triple digits. The problem was that I was laying down rules, but not boundaries.

Reasoning with the Unreasonable

It's time to get real. Someone in your home is a drug user, but you may afraid to do something about it. You don't want to set rules that may alienate you from your loved one. And boundaries, what's the difference? There is a difference between rules and boundaries. Rules are easy to set. Just state your rule and every reasonable person in the room follows. But the challenge is in the term *reasonable*. You see, it can easily be assumed that most everyone is reasonable, but what about the addict in the room? Like I described in early chapters, the chemically-altered brain as a rule has poor reasoning capabilities. It's as if a metaphorical switch has shut off that portion of the brain that controls reasoning capabilities. Highlight this one: *Addicts rarely respond to reason.*

Boundaries are not rules. Boundaries are designed to structure a relationship when rules do not apply or are not relevant to one party. Boundaries are a delineation of where one stands and where one is not willing to go in a relationship and are set with sound and reasoned thought. There is no reason to become angry when setting boundaries. Just state your case, discuss it respectfully, and tape it anywhere visible. Then be prepared to follow-through when your boundaries are not respected. That's the hard part.

Fear of Following Through

The problem with following through is that people feel they risk losing that person's love. It becomes easier for some parents to do nothing and not make any waves. (*"Leave him alone. He'll grow out of it."*) This is nothing more than enabling behaviors evolving into codependency. Parents who show signs of codependency often feel that it is much better to bite the bullet and deal with a crippled and addicted teen who will *never* leave them rather than having a healthy successful one *who might.* There are other fear factors to consider:

- Fear of cutting off the relationship with their loved one. Like I previously stated what relationship?

- Fear of losing one's loved one to the streets. (*Right now, maybe that's where he needs to be.*) Your loved has little interest in warm sheets and those great BLTs you make for him. Homelessness is the result of the choices he has made. And he will live that way until *he* makes a decision to change. You cannot give him a place to sleep as long as he continues to live the using life.

- Fear of displeasing the white elephant in the room. Confronting an addicted loved one about his problem almost always results in verbal abuse from the addict and mental anguish for the parent. You don't need this form of abuse.

- Fear that his friends will abandon him. News flash: they already have. He has wronged many people and they don't want a stoner or a drunk around them. They're moving on to greater things (college, work, etc).

- Fear that your loved one will wind up in jail for a drug related crime. Symptoms of drug use almost always include illegal behavior. Face up to it. If your teen committed a crime, he must do the time. This could be his moment of clarity; his rock bottom. Don't bail him out.

- Fear that your loved one will turn to prostitution. That may be a choice, but a choice made only by the addicted person alone. There is a strong relationship between substance abuse and prostitution. One third of female addicts (and an increasing number of males) supports their habit by working as prostitutes. The addiction is so strong that one is willing to risk HIV, physical abuse or even death for the drug of choice.

- Fear of suicidal threats *("If you don't loan me the money, I'll...")*. Never take a suicidal threat lightly. Hopefully, when your loved one threatens you with suicide that it is nothing more than a display of bravado and a sign of intimidation on the part of the addict. Addicts always make threats when things aren't going their way. Teens especially, believe that all they have to do is play the suicide card and their parents will jump out of their skin. Still, handle this one with caution.

A Healthier You

The purpose of setting boundaries is to take care of ourselves; to show that we have self-worth. No one deserves to be treated abusively. No one deserves to be lied to, manipulated, or betrayed. We all deserve to be treated with respect and dignity. But if we do not respect ourselves enough to stand up to the abuse of our addicted loved ones, and if are afraid to begin breaking old patterns and adopting new ones, then we can never expect them to change their behaviors. We have then made the choice to remain in a toxic environment, and never break away from the ensnaring net called codependency. And that is a sad option.

To Change Others, Change Yourself
"When patterns are broken, new worlds emerge"
(Spanish proverb)

If the fears listed in the last chapter mirror your situation, then it's time for you to draw the line. In our efforts to change others, there is often a strange resistance to change ourselves. We think, *"Why should I change? I'm not the one who's addicted."* We were caught in a parent-trap of *"I'll parent them when they're good and you parent them when they're bad."* In our situation, I was the good guy, the pushover you could negotiate with, while my wife was the wicked witch, the villainous enforcer. It became clear that we could not have one set of rules when mom was around, and another when dad was in the room. It would be bad for our teen, and worse for our marriage. Al-Anon's Three C's now began to make more sense. Although we didn't cause his addiction, we couldn't control it, and we certainly couldn't cure it, there was one thing we could control however, and that was the way we would respond to our teen's addiction from that day forward.

DRAWING THE LINE

Wake up and smell the coffee. You're being held hostage by a person that lies and steals from you even though he says he loves you. He makes promises that he'll seek help; while you sense deep down he won't. *(Addicts are unable to keep promises. They may sincerely wish to, but their disease prevents them from following through.)* You cannot leave him in your home alone for one minute. The grief he has caused has becomes unbearable. Do you wait until you lose your position of worth to your loved one's addiction or do you cut him out of the family constellation altogether?

Some families spend thousands of dollars going from rehab to rehab trying to get their loved one's life back only to realize that their relationship with their drug of choice is stronger than any love of family or friends.

We were at war with a powerful enemy. We had no choice but to fight back as by now we had been left with broken hearts and shallow pockets. Our son's behavior had become so intolerable that disconnection and detachment were our only options. We needed to disconnect from the source of the addictive behaviors and do it in a manner that protected our self-respect and our sanity. Back in the day it was called tough love, and something that today is in need of rediscovery. My father used to say that consequences often were the best teacher. Each time I had a close call (and I've my share) he would say, "*A close call is greater than the best advice.*" Allowing your son to lose his job or is made to sleep in jail for a few nights, can often work miracles. It is about letting your loved one know you care, but that you will stand your ground. Once you have gotten tired of going from one crisis to another and have thrown all the interventions at him that have failed, it is time to back off and let consequences take over.

On the surface, drawing the line or walking away from a bad situation may seem cruel, uncaring or weak. On the contrary, walking away from a toxic situation is all about being strong and able to set personal boundaries for ourselves and having the courage to change a sudden and potentially toxic pattern. In our family's situation, we had to take a hard look at what we were doing and begin asking ourselves, "*Is this what we want?*"

We had to mentally detach from the psychological consequences of our son's addiction, not because we were weak, but because we had a need to protect our sanity, and rebuild our strength.

For us, changing a downward spiraling pattern was the healthiest thing we could have done for ourselves and for our son. Detachment meant having to avoid engaging emotionally in a way that would let our son know we meant business while at the same time protecting our integrity as parents. It meant grabbing the bull by the horns and gaining control over our emotional responses to the damaging aspects of our son's behaviors. Because addiction feeds on drama, detachment meant staying cool and saying, *"We love you, but you've made your choices, and now we're making ours."* With addicted loved ones, boundaries have to be set (and enforced) calmly, respectfully, and without anger, simply because drug dependent teens can quickly turn into loud, disrespectful, strangers when presented with threats and poorly designed boundaries.

TRAPS TO AVOID WHEN SETTING BOUNDARIES:

1. Don't let boundaries inconvenience or hurt you. Setting boundaries should require some manner of creativity so that it doesn't hurt you more than it hurts your teen. Grounding a kid into next year, for example, is also grounding yourself by having to supervise him at all times, thus robbing other members of the family of their quality time with you.

2. Don't be a drill sergeant: The primary role of a drill sergeant is to ensure submission. Drill sergeants often communicate by using threats, punishment,

3. and ridicule such as: *"What is wrong with you? How long are you going to be a stoner?"* The message your kid gets from this type of abuse is that it's not safe to come to you for help or support because more than likely he will be ridiculed and demeaned.

4. Seeking revenge: Naturally, your loved one's addiction has upset the whole family constellation and you're beyond angry. Don't play the "get even" card: *"Let's give him a taste of his own medicine."* Focus on the problem, not on yourself and don't take things personally. Always try to separate the addiction you hate from the person you love.

5. Making idle threats or promises: Desperate parents are often in the practice of threatening or promising: "If you don't stop using..." or "If you bring us four negative U.A.s (urine analysis) you can have your car back." Both methods often fail because first, addicted people don't respond to threats. Remember that you have logged in a history of rescuing and covering up his drug use. Who's going to believe you now? It's almost too late. Second, parents often try to extract and force promises from their loved ones. That doesn't work either because addicts cannot follow through. Their addiction won't let them. The best your kid will do is to try to negotiate you out: *"But I got 3 out of four negative U.A.s. isn't that enough?"*

6. Shaming: When your child makes a mistake he may feel guilty. But when he feels he *is* a mistake, he feels shame. A good example of this is using de-humanizing language, name-calling or making threats of physical abuse (*I'm going to beat you into next Sunday if...*," and humiliating him in front of friends or family members.

7. Don't accommodate the disease. This refers to being held hostage by someone else's addiction. Examples of accommodation include: adjusting your work schedule to supervise your loved one; not taking trips with your spouse for fear of not being available for the addict; going to early shows and dinner so as to return home before anything happens to the house; and not inviting guests over for fear that he might cause embarrassment to himself or you.

8. Repeating or over-emphasizing consequences: Over-emphasizing consequences takes away from the positive aspects of treatment or recovery.

Bottom line: You need to focus on your own life and responsibilities. It is important to reclaim your life before the disease holds you hostage. You should be behind their loved one's recovery process in positive and supportive ways, of course, but you must also be tactful and straight-forward in setting boundaries. Do not expect (or insist) your loved one make sudden changes overnight. Forcing things to happen too quickly will tend to make him more rebellious and unresponsive to treatment.

As in the wars of old, we had to outline the rules of engagement and they had to be consistent and firm. Setting boundaries is not an easy thing to do. Doing it with detachment is twice as hard. That is why you should seek help, advice and counsel from other people who have gone through the same thing, as their experience can benefit you directly. Like it or not, I'm telling you the truth; codependents who go it alone and believe that what they are doing is being done in the name of unconditional love, soon become martyrs to their loved one's cause. Their intentions are good, but good intentions always have a way of backfiring.

Your efforts to rescue go ignored or unappreciated by your loved one whose only goal is to connect with the next high. Below are some action steps you can take to get a foothold in this battle you are in. And as in any war, you will have to adopt tactics that may seem cruel, but necessary:

Action Steps

1. Don't allow your addicted loved one to blame you for his addiction. This nothing more than common manipulation. Unless you have personally injected him with chemicals or put a pipe in his mouth and lighting it, you are in no way at fault.

2. Don't give cash to an addict. He'll just spend it on drugs.

3. It is never a good idea to give an addict anything of great value. It'll just wind up at a pawn shop.

4. Do not do anything for an addict that he cannot do for himself when clean and sober. Doing so makes you a codependent.

5. Hesitate before believing what an addict is saying. It is better to maintain a *show me* posture.

6. Don't rescue; walk away with respect. Conduct yourself with integrity.

7. Don't get engaged in yelling matches or emotionally charged conversations.

8. Let your loved one experience the embarrassment, shame, guilt and consequences of his behavior.

9. Don't get caught up in the drama. Addiction and drama seem to often go hand-in-hand.

10. Don't think that because you are the one that your loved one calls on the phone the most means he loves you. Addicts need money and you may be the easy mark he goes after and not your spouse who is harder to draw money from.

11. Listen respectfully to your addicted loved one. You just may be the only stable and rational person in their life right now. If you can't listen to him without judgment, then who will? You may be his only lifeline now, and in the future.

SETTING REASONABLE BOUNDARIES

"Boundaries tell us who we are."
(Robert Burney)

The word "boundary" is often used to describe physical and emotional limits in relationships. A boundary lays out in clear language what will be acceptable or not tolerated in relationships. You need your loved one to understand that using was his choice and that you are there for support if he decides to make moves towards sobriety, but that you will not be used as a doormat. You want to help him and be there for him, but he must treat you with respect, and you will do the same for him.

1. There are basically two parts to a boundary: 1) describing the behaviors you find unacceptable; 2) A description of the actions you will take to protect the boundary you have set and the extent you will go to enforce it. You must be clear and respectful when setting boundaries. Your loved one can become exceptionally hostile when feeling he is being attacked.

ACTION STEPS

2. Remember the Three C's as you consider setting your boundaries.
3. Be honest with yourself about a loved one's addiction. It is what it is.
4. Work together with other family members when making boundary decisions.
5. Value yourself. The only people who appreciate a doormat are those with dirty shoes.
6. Be selfish. Self-preservation is the key to a healthy balance.
7. Remember that your safety and the safety of other family members are important. Do not use a shaming and blaming voice when setting boundaries.
8. Do not dredge up past issues with your loved one. An addict lives in the *here* and *now* and must be dealt with here and now language.

9. Limit your time with the addict so that you can be with other family members.
10. Participate in a support group with other families experiencing the same crisis.
11. Be a supportive partner. This sickness takes a toll on everyone and if one partner is inconsistent, you are then fighting two battles alone.
12. Make *NO* your favorite word. It's small; it just has two letters, but it's oh so powerful.

In part, the goal in setting boundaries is to inconvenience the addict so much so that he either changes his behavior, enrolls in a treatment program, or leaves. Remember the goal is not to win, but to communicate that you mean business and to save your sanity. Never make hollow threats or rules you cannot enforce. It is also important that your spouse agrees with the boundaries and is prepared to enforce them also. Standing as a united front as parents is crucial when you are fighting against a foreign substance that has invaded your loved one's brain. Ten reasonable boundaries come to mind:

1. Curfews: You and other family members need the rest, therefore there has to be a time set when all doors will be locked and no one gets in.
2. Language: Swearing, disrespectful comments, yelling, and foul language will not be tolerated.
3. Influencing other family members: Addicts need using and drinking buddies and where better to recruit than from one's own family.
4. Not serving as a chauffeur to the addict (middle of the night pickups).
5. Cell phone use: Addicts need to call their drug hook-ups. Have your loved one pay for his phone and usage. When his minutes run out and he's short on cash, oh well.
6. Car restrictions: If he drives a car you have insured and he's still boozing and using, put a boot on his steering wheel and cancel his insurance until he can sober up and pay for it himself.
7. Having strangers in the home: This is your family home and must be respected by people who visit. Sketchy characters should not be allowed.

8. Borrowing personal items: Addicts lose or sell items for drugs. Our son went through three cell phones, a laptop, an Ipad, two sets of earphones, and my best leather jacket.
9. Keeping track of his appointments: If he misses a court date, tough luck.
   Lying to his county or school officials: If an official calls you, be honest.
10. Covering up for your child sends a message that you're conspiring with him thus allowing him to keep on using.

How many more can you add:_____

_____

_____

_____

_____

_____

_____

Don't Add Fuel to the Fire

Keep the lines of communication open. Always buffer your bottom line with a loving statement that keeps the door open to recovery: "...*until you seek help.*" But don't get fooled by claims of being abstinent. Just because your loved one hasn't had a drink in the last couple of days or weeks doesn't mean he's in recovery, and are not good reasons to remove the boundaries you have set. Adopt a *show me* position in cases like these. Recovery means visiting a professional, a licensed alcohol and drug counselor, or enrolling in an   treatment facility. Anything beyond that is just plain manipulation.

Never engage in any arguments or shouting matches. I easily fell into that trap. Reacting in this manner with your teen only fuels the fire. Addicts (teens especially) can be manipulative and have an uncanny way of turning an issue back to you. When you react by exploding, you take the focus off of them, and put it right on you. Then you become the bad guy, giving your teen yet another excuse to continue using.

Effective Boundary Statements

Getting tough on a loved one *is* about love. It is the greatest display of love a parent can give to a child. As you practice these boundary statements, don't forget to add a buffer statement: *"...until you seek and accept professional help."* at the end of each statement.

- *"I will no longer give you money until you seek professional help."*
- *"You can no longer live in our home unless you seek and accept professional help.*
- *"I'm taking the car away until you get help for your alcohol problem."*
- *"I've pretended not to notice your problem in the past. From now on, if you come over when you are high, you will not be welcomed in our home."*
- *"The next time I see you get in a car while intoxicated, I will call the police."*
- *"You can no longer work in the family business until you get help."*
- *"I'm not going to tell your boss you have the flu when you have a hangover."*
- *"Your mom and I will no longer pay for your school expenses until you get help."*

(Sources: Intervention Services Inc.; S.M.A.R.T. Model of Interventions.)

Signs That Your Boundaries Aren't Working

1. You're constantly telling and reminding him what to do.
2. You constantly preach, beg, plead and bribe for a change in behavior.
3. You're consistently warn, lecture, sermonize, and threaten.
4. You do tasks for him because you're too tired, busy or simply want to just keep the peace and move on.
5. You keep bringing up past examples of what he did wrong.
6. You compare him to other, more successful siblings or friends.
7. You provide solutions even when they are not solicited.
8. You're whining daily about what he should and shouldn't do.
9. You criticize.
10. You create guilt trips.

LETTING CONSEQUENCES HAPPEN

"Sooner or later everyone sits down to a banquet of consequences."
(Robert Louis Stevenson)

We finally reached the point where we had had enough. We began to look for ways to fight back the anger and guilt that had welled up inside us. It was time to regain our strength and pay attention to other family members who had begun to avoid us. We followed Wayne Dyer's advice from his lectures and book, *The Shift* by modifying (or shifting) our old irrational thinking to a more practical way of looking at this problem. We began shifting from a *we can't* position to a more positive *we can,* and from a notion of *we're stuck,* to one of *we're free.* We modified the popular Al-Anon Three C's mantra in that we could not change or control his addiction, but we sure as hell could manage and control our reaction to it. We refused to allow our son's choices to define who we were as a family. It was what it was and we just had to deal with it, and at the end of the day, isn't this the beginning of healing?

Take Care of Number One

Getting angry can be healthy and perfectly normal in situations like this, but don't dwell on it. You must first take care of yourself during this trying period. If you don't take care of yourself first, how do you expect to take care of those around you who are also being affected by this crisis? An airplane analogy comes to mind. Picture yourself on an airplane with the flight attendant instructing you to put on your oxygen mask first before helping others. It's a no-brainer. If you don't put on your oxygen mask first before doing anything else, then neither you nor the person next to you may survive the emergency.

But if you take care of yourself first, you will be in a better position to take care of others who are still around and desperately need your help.

Action Steps

Responsible parents try to focus on their health and sanity first. Then they can focus on the needs of the other family members. Below are ten action steps that were shared with us that will increase the likelihood that you'll address your crisis in a rational and healthy manner:

1. Remain positive and in good spirits each time you speak with your loved one. You have every right to be in good spirits.

2. Keep reminding your loved one that there is help and when he chooses to accept it, you can take him there, and in some cases (considering the age and size of the child, for example) you may just have to put him in your car and take him to get the help he needs whether he wants to or not.

3. If violence is an issue, there are treatment facilities that will personally come and take your teen from your home on your behalf. In the long run he will thank you.

4. Focus on the three R's: Regroup (meet regularly as a family unit with other family members), Reassess (discuss how each is coping) and Rebuild (do fun and positive things). Never forget the needs of other family members.

5. Try not to argue over finances. Treatment can be very expensive and can quickly splinter a family.

6. Support each other as spouses by not allowing your loved one's addiction to weaken the relationship. Make it known that this is only temporary and you have not given up on each other.

7. Walk, run, swim, garden…just keep moving. Then do it some more. To quote Dr. Phil, *"No dog ever peed on a moving car."* Jog or take walks together. It's amazing how quickly exercising frees up the mind, and when the endorphins kick in, it causes one or both spouses to become a bit more reasonable in discussions relating to their crisis.

8. Read, meditate or pray. Better yet, do all three. Free your imprisoned mind. Ask your Creator (or personal Higher Power) to keep your loved one safe and your family sane. Then give thanks for any blessing that comes your way.

9. Find a trusted and unbiased ear that can support you unconditinally. You may need to talk to someone who will let you vent and allow the painful details of the crisis to pour out e.g., what happened, your thoughts on why it happened, and how the crisis is affecting you.

10. Don't take your family crisis to work. Leave your baggage in the parking lot. Seventy-five percent of your coworkers don't really care about your problems, and the other Twenty-five percent are glad you have them.

(*Sources: Alcoholics Anonymous, Al-Anon/Alateen, the generous people at the National institute on Drug Abuse for Teens and the works of Beverly Conyers and Melodie Beattie.*)

LETTER TO MY SON: Week Twelve

"Spirituality is not about doing, but about being."
(Earnie Larsen)

Hello son:

How are things going for you in Hotel California? For us, it is a overcast and breezy Sunday afternoon, and the sun has barely made its cameo appearance. Remember how it would get grey and the leaves on the trees would begin to turn color and fall to the ground? It's like that today, a blanket of red and gold everywhere. The chilly wind is beginning to blow, forcing us to zip up our jackets a little tighter. There is no question that fall is in the air. It is pot roast weather once again. Remember our Sunday dinners. I can't wait until we are all together at the dinner table once again. This evening I will start our last bonfire in our fire pit and think of the good times that will come once you are out. You and I seem to be alike in that we both enjoy peace, nature and the value of a good campfire. Life is starting to feel good once again.

As I sit on the porch with my laptop, I hear a hawk screeching in the trees and as I look to locate his perch, my mind wanders off to the times you would be outside by the fire pit inspecting a small rodent that had perhaps scurried away from the fire and as you paused to marvel at an apple on our tree that was providing its yearly feast to all the birds in the neighborhood. There is an ancient quotation that reminds me of you: *"Smile, breathe, go slowly and see the Creator at work."* That is the person I've come to know in you: One who observes everything as a special gift from God; one who does things at his own pace and finds value in every little moment; at every living thing.

Getting back to the business at hand, I have read several of your letters and have listened carefully to your concerns during our rushed, long distance telephone conversations about being moved to a different section and feeling that you don't belong there. I suspect they do that for two reasons: Safety, and to screw with your mind. I sense you are sick and tired of this new psychic load you've been carrying, say nothing of having to deal with the anxiety attacks you've admitted you get nightly. I can only imagine the pain you must be going through. But I'm not going to debate with you any more about whether you belong there or not. You know what you did and why you are there. It is something you will have to deal with yourself. It is what it is, and there is little you or I can do anything about.

All I can tell you is what you can do to never return:

First, think for a moment about what you did that got you there. Then think about how much your addiction hurt you as you looked over your shoulder, running from the police. Think of those thorny bushes where you hid, with your arms bleeding from the cuts. Think how those cuffs felt at four o'clock in the morning as you sat in a police station, shivering, exhausted and hungry. Think of the nightly anxiety attack you endured while locked up. Always keep fresh in your mind the baggy, orange jumpsuit and how you felt the times you had to physically defend yourself from physical harm. Think of sleeping with one eye open each night because you didn't trust the inmate you now had for a cellmate. And finally, think of the processed meat and expired milk you had to eat and drink on a daily basis in an 8x10 cell with only recycled air to breathe for 360 days.

Never forget the pain of all that, son. Keep those visions at the forefront of your mind at all times as it is an important memory you must never lose. Because it is that memory, hopefully, that will keep you from relapsing or violating a section of your probation that will cause you to go back. You now have only one option: to hang tough and devise a good plan for yourself. Work a good aftercare program while locked up and after you are released, or for damn sure son, <u>you will relive those one thousand deaths all over again.</u>

You have also expressed that you are frightened and unsure of what you will become from this whole experience. I get it. You wonder if you will become a bitter man and come out in worse shape than when you went in. Those thoughts are natural. It is hard for me to answer these questions for you. Let me take this time to talk about this a little more.

First, I agree with you when you say that you will come out of this experience a changed man, but what you haven't considered is that if you remain focused and work a good program for yourself, you will undoubtedly come out a stronger and wiser man. I know this because you have had two pretty solid teachers in your mother and me, along with several great role models in your extended family. Even though you tripped yourself up, our conversations during my visits with you still indicate to me that you understand what good character means. Just know that even people with good character make mistakes and must get back on track. You just got temporarily blown off course.

Second, although what has happened to you as a result of your crime is very serious, it is only a disruption in your life, and like I said, a storm that blew you off course. Even when you have been released and in treatment, you will find that you will be faced with problems; some of which will be serious, while others less so. Some will be your fault and some not. It doesn't matter. The point is problems are not the problem, but how you deal with them is; especially in your first year out and while in recovery. That is where the real challenges will lie. That is why a strong and continuous program will be of critical importance to you. Find one, build one, and stick to it.

So to answer your question about you being in a storm, the word "storm" in this case is just another word for the adversity you are currently facing. The good thing about adversity is that it has a tendency to change people, making us more resilient, stronger, wiser and more prepared for the next storm. That process is called: *building character*. So don't get down on yourself just because you made a mistake. Don't let your jail experience define you. Remember that adversity doesn't define a person; it is how one handles adversity that defines us. Never forget this.

Is your life now ruined and beyond repair? No. Can the addictive brain be repaired? Yes. Is it going to be easy? No. It's going to take discipline, a good aftercare program, and some heavy lifting, mostly by you. It's going to require your adoption of new habits; habits that may cause you to become frustrated and make you long for the old and destructive ways of coping. It's an imperfect world, son. But like I said, that's life and life brings us many challenges, both physically and emotionally. And it is these challenges that can often weigh us down if not dealt with early and effectively. There is a quote by Maya Angelou which says it all, *"It's not the load that brings us down, it is the way we carry it."*

Finally, I also feel your concerns about what people will think once you are out. As far as our family is concerned, you won't have to prove anything to us. For those of us who know and love you, no explanation is necessary. For those who don't know you like we do, no explanation is ever going to be enough.

So why bother beating yourself up over what people are going to think?

Those thoughts are a big waste of energy. The only thing I have left to say in this letter is that the life you were living while drugging is not your life's path. Just know that we love you very much, and want you to continue staying positive and strong. We've got your back!

Until we fish again, stay at peace where you are at.

Love, Dad.

HOLDING THE LINE ALSO MEANS LETTING GO

"Get on the bus Gus. Drop off the key Lee..."
(Paul Simon)

Getting Dylan to consider treatment was a major struggle that went nowhere. Nothing made my palms sweat more than when we had to kick Dylan out of our home. Dr. M. Scott Peck said in his book, *The Road Less Traveled* that life is "difficult". That's an understatement as he did not have an addict living in his home. Like many other parents of addicts, I took the easy road; accepting my teen's repeated apologies and me just going along with fingers crossed, hoping that with these apologies and promises, there would come a change. It didn't take long to discover that I was REALLY living with an addict and Dylan's addiction would not allow him to keep any promises. This, Dr. Peck, is the road less traveled.

Living with an addict and dealing with his problems on a day to day basis is just not workable. You have to grab this raging bull by the horns or get gored to death. Dramatic? Maybe. You can continue the denial and enabling and see where that takes you or you can hold the line and show the addict that his actions are harming the whole family and that he needs to get the proper help or leave. In our case, we had to act for better or for worse. Sometimes we must just trust that our decisions are wise. And if they aren't, we try harder next time; and that folks, is the road less traveled.

My wife, finally becoming fed up with my making deals with our son that kept being broken, came home one day with several shipping cartons.

She then methodically began packing all our son's belongings and set the cartons on the front porch. Our family counselor had pointed it out rather succinctly: if an addicted person living in your home refuses to seek help, he must then find another place to live. That was our first lesson in boundary setting. What then is a boundary? For us, it was hardening our hearts. It was drawing a line in the sand.

My wife and I are not strong advocates of booting kids from their home. While addiction and refusing treatment may warrant kicking your teenager out, this is not something that should ever be entered into lightly, or without great consideration for the consequences. Still one must do what is necessary to regain some order in one's life. Below is a list of possible reasons for your loved one to make arrangements to find another place to live:

GET ON THE BUS GUS...

1. Threats of violence. That is the number one reason for making your loved one move out. If you fear for your safety and that of your family's, then he has overstayed his welcome.
2. Undue stress. If his addiction is causing you more visits to the doctor, increased doses in your medications, and feelings of sadness and depression most of the time, then it's time to place him on the "adios" program.
3. If your property is being destroyed or has turned into Swiss cheese from all the holes in your doors and walls, he's got to go.
4. Personal property is missing. Addicts need money to feed their habit. The obvious place to find cash, jewelry, and credit cards is in your home.
5. Your loved one is a bad influence on other family members. Stoners love to be around other stoners and will seek out and recruit siblings or other relatives.
6. You can no longer keep up with the lies. Addicts lie and make promises they just can't keep; plain and simple. How many times has he announced that this is the last time he will use?
7. You're facing financial consequences because the cost of keeping up with your loved one's addiction is going through the roof: jail costs, bail bonds, getting the car out of impound lots, and replacing lost cell phones because you feel it's important to know where your teen is at all times. Really?!
8. You've grown tired of giving him one last chance, and another, and another, and he has blown it each time. If this describes you, then the boy has got to go.

9. You've become weary from tripping over drug paraphernalia and booze bottles in the home after repeated discussions against it.
10. His refusal to go into treatment. As long as you keep providing food and shelter, he's not going anywhere, and why should he?

Stop feeling guilty. Changing the course of events is hard, but necessary. Removing your loved one from your home is never a pleasant task. It works against your parental instincts (to house and protect). In our case, we were confusing the teen we loved with t he addiction we hated. They are not the same. In your case, you must differentiate between the teen you love and the addiction you don't. Then, and only then, can you make a solid decision to evict your loved one. We made it clear to our son that only the sober Dylan was welcomed in our house and that our home was off limits to the addicted Dylan. He seemed to understand what that meant, and soon began loading his boxes into his friend's car. We were lucky, as our son was pretty compliant and very resourceful.

But if there have been violent outbreaks in your home, it may be safer to solicit the help of law enforcement or a relative to assist you. Then you can begin changing the code to the garage door opener and locking down every entry to your home.

When the Guilt Sets In

He's gone, but don't get too comfortable. That *thank-God-he's-gone* feeling is short-lived. I recall finding ourselves worried stiff after we had evicted our son from our home. We became consumed by both guilt and fear. Guilt over what we had to do, and did; and fear because we did not know if our son was safe wherever he was living. His phone had run out of minutes and we had lost contact with him. Our minds and imagination began to play tricks on us: Maybe we made a mistake; maybe he's sitting in a mall confused and helpless; maybe he's injured somewhere in a sketchy part of town. The decisions that we felt were so right, were now being fed back to us as all wrong. A brain filled with negativity can become an unhealthy one in short order.

My first instinct was to punish myself for being so cold and unfeeling. I mean, what kind of a parent walks away from their own child? My second response was to get in my car and find him, bring him back and reach out to him one more time to try and cut one final deal that would change his thinking. It bordered on madness. If I couldn't reach him before, what made me think I could reach him this time? If he wasn't in treatment where he belonged, then frankly there was nothing to negotiate. As I went through our basement repairing the aftermath of his addiction, it dawned on me that we had not really evicted our son; in reality we had evicted an addicted stranger.

FINDING THE RIGHT TREATMENT FACILITY

"You can check out anytime you want...but you can never leave."

(The Eagles)

All the pressure you've put on your kid to clean up his act is starting to pay off. He has finally agreed to participate in a treatment program, and now the hard part begins: locating the right drug rehab facility. Will an in-patient facility work or does he do outpatient? Depending on age, the job of seeking help still rests solely on him. It's his life.

In the interest of time, (and knowing that he might never take the initiative), we had to strike while the iron was hot before he could change his mind. His mother and I took it upon ourselves to spend hours on the Internet and on the phone exploring every option open to him. We asked everyone in the prevention business for the best advice as to how to find the best rehab facilities. Almost all of the admission reps had contradicting suggestions, and all claiming a 90% or greater success rate. We finally selected the clinic that told us, *"There are no guarantees, but let's give it a try."*

Then there are the fees associated with these places. At one end are the exclusive, up-scale centers which offer equine therapy, acupuncture, yoga with the local maharishi and promise tennis with the stars. Who's got that kind of money? Our son is neither a rock star nor the son of a millionaire. Some of the mid-range treatment facilities we contacted were as pushy as used car salesmen, promising state-of-the-art treatment, and meditation field trips to local beaches: *treatment-by-sea*. At the other end of the treatment continuum are the county-funded, grassroots operations run by the state and non-profits that provide minimum services (a cot and a meal), and maybe a little circle time with a counseling intern.

Then there are the procedural questions to deal with. What is *sober living* housing and which type is best for our son? Then there are the faith-based centers where religious learning and chapel services are held to help the person grow spiritually. There are many other options available as well, but these are the most basic.

Location is an important consideration for treatment. Selecting a treatment facility close to home is going to be very helpful. This journey has shown us that addiction is something that affects the whole family and treatment facilities almost always stress the importance of family involvement. You may be asked to attend family counseling sessions and the more you are involved, the more it will help you understand and deal with the nature of addiction.

Then there is the matter of selecting a treatment philosophy your loved one will find most comfortable. In researching treatment philosophies we found those with 12-Step programs were the most common, and form the core of AA. We were told that the 12-Step program provides a clear framework (a blueprint) for an addict to follow during treatment and his ongoing recovery after treatment. We also learned that young addicts often need to combine 12-Step with some form of *Cognitive therapy*, a process for identifying, analyzing, and questioning one's irrational thinking patterns, and begin developing a more rational and healthier way of thinking and dealing with life's stressors. In other words, adopting new habits and techniques which can reinforce doing things differently than what the client was doing when he was using.

It is important for the family to visit the facility to check out the clinical climate. Is it orderly? Does the facility have a welcoming and nurturing environment?

You'll quickly learn whether the place feels right to you or to your teen. Speak to staff and get a feel for the facility. This will help answer any remaining questions you and your teen may have and ensure both of you are making the correct decision. The bottom line is that there is no exact science in choosing a treatment facility. In the end, you've got to trust your intuition. Once you've done all your research (and your teen has done his) and have asked all the questions, your intuition and that of your teen, will be the ultimate judge. Still, taking the time to ask the right questions can save you time, money and a lot of heartache.

The following page offers families a sample list of reasonable questions that could be asked when considering a drug treatment facility.

QUESTIONS TO ASK A TREATMENT FACILITY

1. Is this a licensed facility? How is it accredited? What is the refund policy?

2. What is the therapeutic orientation or philosophy of the program?

3. What is the screening protocol for treatment?

4. What types of assessments are done and who administers them and what are their qualifications?

5. How many hours of individualized therapy or counseling do clients receive weekly and what are the credentials of those conducting that service?

6. What are the topics addressed in the psychotherapy group sessions?

7. Are clients required to acquire a sponsor while in the program and how does a client acquire one while in the program?

8. Does the facility include family members as part of the treatment plan?

9. Does the program offer any kind of personalized relapse prevention planning?

10. Have your teen make a list of the questions he or she may want to ask. It is important that your teen participate in this exercise since he is the one that will be spending time healing.

(Source: *Transitions Recovery Program. Miami Florida.*)

Treatment Programs to Avoid

In our search for treatment programs for our son, we quickly learned that there are some programs that practice policies that do an addicted client more harm than good and they include:

1. Programs that do not subscribe to a mix of 12-Step and Strengths-based coaching. Because adolescents have underdeveloped brains, and come to treatment with cognitive distortions (faulty thinking), they need the benefits of both a 12-step and a strength-based program that can help them sort out their addictive thinking patterns and learn how to self-manage their lives.
2. Programs that mix adolescents with adults. Adults and adolescents have different ways of thinking and mixing them together has not proven to be very effective.
3. Programs that claim an 80-90 percent success rate. This simply does not happen in the real world of treatment. Besides, most treatment programs do not do have an aftercare follow-up component so where's the proof?
4. A program that is punitive in nature. These are programs like boot and wilderness camps that punish kids mentally and physically or have overly harsh restrictions.
5. Programs that are ambiguous about what they do. These are programs that keep parents in the dark and do not require or encourage family participation.

(Source: Tammy Bell: *Preventing Adolescent Relapse.*
CENAPS Model of Treatment.)

THERE IS LIGHT AT THE END OF THE TUNNEL

"Don't despair. God has a plan for you."
(Joel Osteen)

As you reach the end of this book, I suspect you're feeling exhausted and worn out. You've already done the things I've suggested; some more than once. Your loved one has completed treatment and a 28 day crash course on relapse prevention. Now that he is out of treatment, you've seen brief periods when things are going well in his life, and he seems to be turning the corner, but don't get discouraged if all that progress comes to a screeching halt. Your loved one may return to substance use after a period of abstinence. Often that's nothing more than a relapse. A relapse can often be a prime feature of addiction recovery, and can be one of the most painful events in a recovering person's life and his family's. It is during the first year of recovery, with the first ninety days being the most critical, that most people who struggle with addiction may experience one or more relapse, but don't give up hope. It can also be a learning experience for your loved one. Many recovered people have taken those unfortunate instances of relapse and turned them into powerful learning experiences that moved them forward in their recovery.

The time to give up hope should never come. Hope, faith, forgiveness, compassion, understanding, nonjudgmental acceptance, and prayer are now the powerful forces you need to hang on to. In his first relapse cycle, your son may still be making progress, and if he has hooked up with an effective and supportive aftercare program that combines 12-Step with cognitive restructuring (*reconstructing self-defeating thoughts and beliefs*) then the chances of a relapse are going to be greatly reduced. And if he relapses again (which he could), I guarantee you that the relapse will be much shorter and less severe because of the training and support he has received.

He is learning to figure it out. If he makes it through the first year of sobriety (even with a relapse or two), the notion of surrendering to cravings and desires will become less attractive and the relapses will decline and ultimately vanish over time. Just know that in recovery there can be a healing pattern: *three steps forward; one step back.* The heartening fact is that if your loved one stays focused on his recovery program and maintains contact with his sponsor, support group, or his outpatient provider, he will begin to experience five steps forward and no steps back. My final message to you is to not give up on yourself or your loved one.

LETTER TO MY SON: Week Twenty-Eight

"Watch your thoughts, for they become words. Watch your words, for they become actions. Watch your actions, for they become character. Watch your character, for it becomes your destiny."

(Buddhist quote)

Good afternoon, son. It is now late November and you know how cold the wind can get. Soon it will be December, the holidays will be upon us, and the snow will be piling up to our waist. But the warm part of this whole thing is that you'll be home around that time.

I understand these last few weeks are going to be challenging for you, with the holidays coming and all. Your girlfriend will be gone with her family and you'll both be cut off from any telephone contact. Mom said her visit with you this month was fantastic and that you look great. We are very appreciative of your positive attitude and how you are handling yourself. We are on the downhill run now, son.

I am happy to hear that you have begun to explore how you got in that place and are expressing how the shortcut you took to make some quick money backfired. There are no shortcuts to anything worthwhile in life, son. Look at those around you and see how well shortcuts worked for them. I'm sure there are hundreds in that facility you're in who chose to take shortcuts all in the name of fun, fame or a little chump change. Then, like a pit bull, life's consequences turned around and bit them in ass. In your case, you took so many shortcuts that at times you must have felt like an octopus on roller skates: a whole lot of movement, but never quite moving forward, backwards or sideways.

Now, as you are looking to get out, you must think how you can walk a different path and break away from the old habits and acquire new ones. It's going to take the same, if not more, hard work that it took to acquire the old, bad habits. They say that there is a lot of comfort and a degree of safety in sticking with old, reliable habits, even though they may be harmful or bad. So take this opportunity son, and learn from your mistakes. Shortcuts? With positive outcomes? Take it from your old man, they're just not out there. I have attached in at the end of this letter a one-page poem by a counseling friend of my entitled: *Life's Lessons in Five Easy Chapters.* Read it and paste it on your wall as you plan your out the rest of your life. I feel reading it is very appropriate at this time. It is about standing back and taking a long, hard look at yourself and what you've done in life, and then devising a better, healthier plan for the future. You may discover that often all it takes is just one short, but impactful decision to change your whole life. If you don't like the road you've been traveling because it's unhealthy for you, then take a different one.

On another note, from your letters and telephone conversations, I'm beginning to feel a positive change in you. You're beginning to open up and admit some of your errors. We are all pleased that you have begun to look at yourself closely and are beginning to explore what it is you need to do to never return to jail. Even in our visits, you seem to have a more mature way of looking at life. That is a good sign of growth. Keep it up.

I'm also beginning to hear hope in your voice, hope that once out, life is still very possible. We are also pleased that things are working out for you. I am pleased to hear that the biblical and spiritual quotations you requested are bringing you the strength you seem to need. I'm pleased to hear that you are beginning to pray.

I have talked to God through prayer myself many times these past months and let me just say that it's crazy. I mean it works. Of course, my motives have been more of a selfish nature. I always ask that He protect you, that He shine his special light on you, that He give you strength and wisdom, and that He keeps your mom and me strong. It is funny how we find God in the darkest crevices of our experiences. No matter. The important thing is that we are in constant communication with Him, and that helps us get through this ordeal.

It has taken courage for me to admit that I have come to love and honor God in my own fashion, not just for what he is doing for you while in that place, but for the love and strength he has given your mother and me and the for power that has brought us closer as a result. It has required courage on our part, and will take the same amount of courage for you to make the right changes that will serve you well out once you are out. Making the right changes and rebuilding your character will take a lot of courage. But be forewarned. Rebuilding one's character doesn't just happen overnight. It doesn't happen by reading new age, philosophical books alone. You have to do it by yourself and with a little help from God, piece by piece, thought by thought, conscious choice by conscious choice. This will no doubt be my last letter until I come to pick you up. Stay strong. I'll see you at the end of the tunnel, son. That is where the light is.

Until we fish again, be at peace where you are at.

Love, Dad.

LIFE'S LESSONS IN FIVE EASY CHAPTERS

Chapter I

I walk down the street. There is a deep hole in the
sidewalk.
I fall in.
I am lost...I am helpless.
But it isn't my fault.
It takes forever to get myself out.

Chapter II

I walk down the same street. There is a deep hole
in the sidewalk.
I pretend not to see it. I fall in again.
I can't believe I am in the same place, but isn't my
fault.
It still takes a long time to get out.

Chapter III

I walk down the same street. There is a deep hole
in the sidewalk.
I see it there.
My eyes are wide open, but I still fall in...it's a
habit.
I know where I am. It is my fault.
I get out immediately.

Chapter IV

I walk down the same street.
There is a deep hole in the sidewalk.
I walk around it.

Chapter V

I walk down a different street.

(From: *There's a Hole in My Sidewalk* by Portia Nelson)

WHAT I'VE LEARNED ABOUT MYSELF

"Only God can take a mess and turn it into a message."
(Joel Olsteen)

Thank you for reading what I've had to say. You could say that experience was a cathartic event of sorts as I found myself melding three emotions at once: 1) reliving the pain as this crisis unfolded; 2) reliving those brief moments of laughter, hope; and 3) experiencing the miracle of patience, hard practice, and love for someone dear to us. But catharsis was not my main reason for writing this.

In writing this book, I hope I have broken the seal of secrecy that exists in many addicted families in that we do indeed play a secret role in our loved one's addiction. We do it quite innocently through silence, denial, enabling and not following through on the boundaries we had set. To repeat an Al-Anon quotation, *"Love that does not include boundaries is not truly love."* Setting boundaries and sticking to them can often be the most loving gesture a parent can make for his teen. Letting him fall on his face and learn from it is another form of unconditional love. I hope I was able to bring this truth out through our story.

This experience has taught me that being too much of an involved parent can be just as counterproductive as not being involved enough. Sometimes helping doesn't help. On the surface, rescuing or solving a dysfunctional loved one's problem may seem like a caring, supportive thing to do, but it is not. Rescuing doesn't do anyone any favors and it's a dishonest act as it robs the teen from learning and growing from his mistakes and causes long-term damage to the parent.

A father can only do his best to protect and guide his children. We can love them, but we can't save them. We cannot orchestrate or manage their destiny.

Everyone has a path in life and I am learning, a little late perhaps, how to get out of the way of our children's path. When it is all said and done, they will live and someday die, with or without our involvement. I wish I had gotten to this realization sooner, but you know what they say about hindsight. Each day that I work on my own codependency issues, I become stronger. I now accept only those challenges that I personally face, rather than the challenges of my children. I work at listening respectfully, but I don't throw out unsolicited advice like rice at an Italian wedding. However, my kids know I am still there for them within healthy limits.

My wife and I are becoming more optimistic of our son's recovery. We are finally relaxing and going to restaurants where you look down at the menu, not up. Meaning that we now have time to relax and talk about things more important to the two of us. Do I ever stop worrying? No, not really. I sometimes catch myself glancing over at the telephone when it rings, hoping that it's not the police, a hospital, or worse. At times, I get this gnawing worry that what happened once before could happen again. But because he lives on his own now, and is figuring stuff out for himself, the worrying is subsiding. Please understand that our family has been to hell and back and, frankly, we're dealing with a cunning, infinitely patient, relentless, disease. It is always in the shadows, waiting for an unguarded moment to pounce. And it is that knowledge that makes me skittish. I have come to learn from this experience, to keep my optimism in check. The progress he has made guarantees nothing. But we've got to trust in our son as he moves forward in recovery. I, too, have to give it my best shot.

One thing I have learned throughout this entire ordeal is that a father can only do the best he can to protect and guide his children.

We can love them, but we can't save them. We cannot orchestrate or manage their destiny. Everyone has a path in life and I am learning, a little late perhaps, how to get out of the way of our children's path. In doing so, they can do what they have to do, and, as parents, we can do what we have to do. When it is all said and done, they will live and someday die, with or without our involvement. I wish I had gotten to this realization sooner, but they say hindsight is 20/20.

So we've come to the end of our story. I so much wanted it to have a fireworks and sparklers happy ending, but that would be unrealistic. Nothing has been easy. We made a lot of mistakes along the way, but we survived and learned from them. We are now able to look back at this year with a detachment that comes with experience and the passing of time. But still, when one's own life is the main actor in a horror movie it becomes difficult to become fully detached. All we can do is look ahead with cautious optimism and thank our Creator for keeping our family together and sane.

The snow has melted now and things are looking up. I'm getting my energy back. I am grateful for a lot of things, but mainly I am grateful that my son is alive and that life, in its harshest form, has something good to teach us. I am also learning to nurture myself more instead of everyone else. My wife and I now go to restaurants where we take our time and look down at a menu instead of up. Like our son, we are learning to live better, one day at a time; doing whatever it takes to make life pleasing in the present, and why not? The best thing about the future is that it too comes one day at a time. Is this the psychic place where parents in our situation wind up? Is this the new normal?

However you use this book, just know that we are all in this fight together, and the only way we're going to win it is to come out of the addiction closet and speak out with courage and determination. Never give up the fight. Our children are worth the effort. With the help of one another, we will be better able to understand and combat this drug pandemic. The only weapon against drugs is *YOU*. Don't give up on your kid, and don't give up on yourself either. Stay healthy and good luck.

Thank you for letting me share our story with you.

Luis D. Velarde, Ph.D.

THIS IS WHERE I GET OFF

""What a long Strange Trip its been."
(The Grateful Dead)

So we've come to the end. As I have alluded, the writing this book was enormously painful. Writing it almost on a daily basis as an excuse for sanity was pure hell.

I have said throughout that I am not an expert on anything, and as a result, cannot judge anyone at any level. I'm just a dad who wishes things had been different. But, have learned through all this that there is no shame in acknowledging that a loved one has a drug problem. Just don't be too hard on yourself.

I've come to agree wholeheartedly with the foremost articles and every rational antidrug campaign that we are finally coming around and saying that drug addiction is an illness. No, a cancer. Yes, I said cancer. The next time you open your newspaper to the obituary page look up someone who has died of cancer and it will almost always say something like, *"After losing a long battle with cancer..."* Addiction is a cancer, and addicts are in a long battle for their lives just like cancer patients. Both illnesses impact an entire family. But addicts don't get the attention and treatment that cancer patients do. Mainly because addicts don't have any clout.

A call to Arms

Addicts are referred to in hushed tones a *secret* shame, treated as proverbial elephants in a room and who are treated as irresponsible, immoral and weak. Amy Winehouse's recent death comes to mind, where we stood by watching the appalling and humiliating behavior her disease caused. Then CNN reran an old piece entitled *"Our favorite bad girls"* We laugh at someone else's pain as we sit in front of our laptops downloading and forwarding Amy Winehouse jokes.

If Amy's behavior had been a result of cancer, we would have treated her differently, but because she was an addict and an alcoholic, she became fair game for comedians and talk show hosts alike.

Cancer has not been eradicated, of course. But more people are alive today because of the investment we have made. What once was a death sentence is now a treatable disease. We need an all out war on addiction just like the lavishly funded war we have waged against cancer and aids. But because the fight against drugs has been waged through archaic policies (interdiction and arrest) and the cost astronomical, the thinking is that we should just call a *cease fire* and legalize certain drugs and move on...the problem is way too big to fight. This is now being supported by the sudden paradigm shifts in national and international drug policies.

Substance abuse must be treated for the cancer that it has become. The same amount of money that it took to put on astronauts on the moon, should be spent on conquering this dreaded disease. To paraphrase the famed cancer research Amelia Arria, have we solved the cancer (and AIDS) problem? NO. Are there less people dying of cancer (and AIDS)? YES.

Just like in cancer and AIDS, a multi-layered approach to eradicating addiction needs to be implemented, one that addresses education, prevention, treatment, aftercare, and changes in public policy (low or no cost accessibility to everyone in need of treatment) all focused on the same goal. The more people know about the disease of addiction, the less stigma will be attached to the individual who suffers from it, and more people will be willing to get the help they need. This is the only way this war must end.

WELCOME TO THE OTHER SIDE:
Message for Teens & Young Adults in Recovery

Now that your sober, what's next?

A Letter to Young Recoverees

"A person recovering on his own is his own worst enemy."
(Earnie Larsen)

Hello:

My name is Dylan, and this long letter is for you; young men and women who have gotten into trouble through alcohol and drugs, and are paying your dues. I believe you are now ready to move forward with a fresh, new life so now that you're sober, what's your next move? As you read my letter you're likely having a whirlwind of thoughts going through your head. Using may have been the most difficult and painful experiences of your life, but looking back you've survived those tough times, some of you more than once. You've experienced God's tap on the shoulder, you've hit rock bottom, and some of you have wound up in jail. Now, you have arrived at a moment of clarity. Great clichés, right? No matter how they say it, these quotes all tell the same story: You were unable to manage your life. Now you've made it to the other side, more or less intact. You've overcome significant hurdles and a lot of pain just to get clean and sober. Congratulations!

You've graduated; you've made it; you're out. But it's not freedom yet. Like me, you find yourself wondering about several things: Where do I go from here? What do I do now with my new life? What are the strategies for staying clean and sober? Your first thought may be to get back on Facebook or Twitter to reconnect with your old gang. Chill out; think this through before doing something crazy. Here are some facts that you can bank on: Those who have been through treatment (or done time), and who have returned to the same old peer group where all the troubles began, almost always fall prey to the revolving door effect, and in a short time relapse or return to jail.

When I came out of jail and a treatment program I was frightened, especially knowing I was being transitioned to the same old school and the same druggies. You're going to find handling that transition a tough road, as well.

I'm a dude who pulls no punches, so please allow me to keep it real. The healing must continue even after treatment. Like me, you are still a young person and may have little or nothing say as to where you will live. You can't move across town or move to Alaska or some faraway place just to stay clean Flash: drugs are everywhere, man. Based on your age, you will more than likely be integrating into the same environment that initially introduced you to alcohol and drugs in the first place. You may find yourself trying to avoid your old using buddies. Staying clean and sober is not going to be easy, but it can be done. For starters, you definitely need a plan. Although the obsession to drink has been removed, difficult people have not. The same losers and haters are right where you left them. Without a solid and carefully constructed strategy for your first days, weeks and months of recovery, you'll not only find yourself fighting an uphill battle, but you will find that you will be tempted around every corner. It won't do you any good to just cruise along day to day hoping for a miracle. You may even relapse, but even that's not the end of the world. It often happens to people without a good recovery plan. But with a good plan and some aftercare support of people who love you, your chances of experiencing a relapse will be reduced.

At the end, I've listed suggestions that have been written by people like you who are in recovery. Now that you're sober, you can use all the help you can get.

Supportive People are More Available Than You Think

There is a saying among folks in recovery that says, "*If you want to stay clean, you must change your playpen and your playmates.*" Meaning, you can't form new and positive habits with the same old using crowd. You must work the program you have been taught 24/7, rain or shine, whether you like it or not. You must now put yourself in new settings, with new and clean friends who support a non-using philosophy. They are the ones who can help you pick up new and practical solutions for dealing with your emotions and frustrations as you interact in your new and sober world. How do you find them? There is an answer for that, and it's a good one.

Begin by spending time with your 12-step sponsor and fellow 12-steppers during the most critical three months of your recovery. They each have been where you are right now: *Early recovery*. They know what an uncertain time this can be, how difficult certain decisions are, how frightening and terrible the future may seem, and how afraid you may be of failure. That companionship and those meetings will now become your rock. You will now be moving in a lifestyle that is going to keep you clean and sober and in a short while you will be creating your own network of recovery support.

THE STRAIGHT TRUTH
I'm giving you the straight truth here, nothing less, because knowledge is power and I now want you to use that power to change the rest of your life.

This bears repeating, transitioning is going to be messy and tough. No one likes to learn new ways of behaving or giving up old friends and habits, but the challenges that come with transitioning will find you needing extra support and care from new and special friends that support sobriety. A person recovering on his own is his worst enemy. Please believe that.

Don't squander the investment you and your family have made. The first thing you must learn is that the friends who once shared your lifestyle did not change their behaviors while you were gone, and there's nothing you can do about that. You cannot expect them to change just because you have. That's madness. There were never any loyalties with this group and they will still pick your pockets the minute your head is turned. Know that! Log this away in your head: You cannot keep the same using friends and expect them to respect your sobriety. They won't. That's like going to a crack house and asking for the *no smoking* section.

Too harsh? Then change what you've been doing. You and your loved ones invested a lot of money, time, and energy to get you where you are today. You are a different person now with your own challenges to deal with. You'll quickly discover that those personal experiences, though painful, have matured you, and when you combine them with what you are learning in aftercare, there is really nothing in common you can share with your old using crowd. You've outgrown them. If you can begin rebuilding and recreating yourself for the better today, and with the right attitude, the proper tools, and a little faith in yourself, you will gain the confidence to remain sober. With the right aftercare support, you'll be moving forward and your past wrongdoings will never come back to haunt you.

Keep your mind right. Stay busy, and just hang in there. You can now begin to take responsibility for your new life and the choices that you will now make. Keep moving forward, and you'll get through this period of transition. I wish you the best and hope everything works out for you.

Have a nice day, unless you have made other plans.

Dylan

YOU'RE ON THE MEND

"You don't like what you're getting? Then change what you're doing."
(Starting Point)

The following suggestions are not the be-all-end-all, but they are easy to do and can help you jump start and maintain your sobriety. When we are Hungry, Angry, Lonely, or Tired, the chances of becoming vulnerable to making poor choices increase. There is a catchy acronym I use with teens and adults in recovery which is called **H.A.L.T.** (*hunger, anger, lonliness, and exhaustion*)Paying attention to these simple needs is an effective way to stop addictive thinking that often triggers using thoughts. Does it end with these needs? No, but just the fact that we are able to identify and address these basic needs is a step in the right direction:

    a. **H**unger – Don't let yourself go hungry. Maintain a healthy eating lifestyle. Your body is your temple. Honor it. When you were using, your body became your first casualty. You may have lost or gained weight, your hair thinned out, your teeth rotted, and you were always hacking and coughing because of all the crap you ingested. Begin keeping yourself clean inside and out.

    b. **A**nger – Try not to let yourself get angry. When you were drinking and drugging, anger was your first response to anything and everything. You walked around chronically pissed off. Get your anger out...but in non-defensive ways. In recovery, not everyone is going to be your best friend. And not everyone will care that you are living sober. Things will now pile up: You have to see your P.O. every week, you have to pee in a cup (random UA's), no one understands your situation, and the slackers and haters are giving you the "stink-eye" as they wait for you to screw up. Just keep your cool. Don't take out your anger out on yourself or on those relationships you value.

c. **L**onliness - Being alone is a sure path to relapse. Highlight this tip: *NEVER* catch yourself being alone or isolated from positive others. Building a new life is not an easy thing. You may have to deal with the leftover baggage from your past and suffer mood swings, ups and downs, and possibly some depression on your sober journey. The fact that you will undoubtedly have to cut yourself from your using relationships will leave you with nagging feelings of loneliness. Get out among healthy people. It's amazing how just getting out and talking it out with others that are in the same situation as you can remind you that you aren't alone in your recovery.

d. **T**iredness – You're off the merry-go-round, now. Take a little time to reflect. Don't let yourself get tired. Remember when you were using? You were running around like an exclamation point on steroids and could not find the time to rest. You were burdened with all your using thoughts and worries: *"Where am I going to get the money to buy more drugs? What am I going to do if I get kicked out of the house? What if I lose my job...? How am I going to get high...?"* and so on until you dropped from exhaustion. You even feared going to bed at night because you couldn't sleep and would find yourself alone with someone you didn't really like: *YOU!* Exhaustion makes a person weak and a weak person becomes more susceptible to feelings of depression and prone to cravings for alcohol or drugs. Chill; learn to relax and have it be okay. Relaxation is an essential part of recovery. Take walks, jog, lift weights or do something more structured like meditation or yoga. Your local YMCA has great programs for getting back in shape and they offer youth rates and some scholarships.

Invest in yourself. Use this time to listen to music *(music that is different than the stoner or slacker musical choices you gravitated to when you were using)*. Get with your Higher Power for a moment and give thanks for another day of sobriety and talk to Him of your plans for tomorrow. Ask him to help stop the endless chatter in your head.

TIME TO CLEAN HOUSE

"One more day that I've survived; another night alone.
Pay no mind I'm doing fine; I'm breathing on my own."
(Foo Fighters)

There is an ancient saying that says, *"The best time to plant a tree was twenty years ago. The second best time is now;"* meaning that it's never too late to renew priorities. While you undoubtedly will encounter times when your mind wanders back to what happened in the past, refocusing your attention to the life you now have is a sign that you recognize you're in recovery. Still, it bears repeating: Stay in the present. Be here, now. What you do today is what matters, not what happened yesterday and not what may possibly happen tomorrow. Focus your attention on your priorities and goals. Be humble, be open to learning new things, and embrace your new life in recovery. It's now time to clean house. Be more involved with your loved ones and show them how much you appreciate them. Express gratitude for their patience. They've also been through a lot.

GET WITH YOUR HIGHER POWER

Someone greater than I (maybe Mark Twain, Thoreau, it's not important) once said: *"Many men go fishing without ever knowing that it wasn't the fish they were after."* You may be wondering, "Why all the spirituality talk and references to God in this book?" Not to get too preachy here, but there is a saying among recovering addicts and alcoholics: *"Let go and let God."* Nothing could be more real. There is no better time to hook up with your Higher Power than now. Express gratitude for the gift of life and your sobriety. Many of us are always willing to share our worse moments of alcoholism or addiction, but few share their spiritual journey. Many find it profoundly embarrassing to talk about the positive changes that have overcome them. Talk about them anyway. What was your moment of clarity?

When did you decide that enough was enough? Share that with others.

Share with them also the wisdom that has now been ushered into your life. Why sit in a circle with strangers, hugging a box of Kleenex while wallowing in your problems, when the solutions and how you found them are much more interesting. Think about it: spirituality and recovery are two powerful processes that go hand-in-hand. It doesn't have to be about religion, but so what if it is. For now, just being connected with your Higher Power should be enough. A good example is my form of spirituality: *fishing*. Fishing is my form of prayer and meditation, and a time for spiritual self-examination. As I sit in my boat I feel a connection with God and the whole living world. It gives me the opportunity to talk to him and being totally reflective in what He has provided our family. That is my time to give thanks for the gift of healing, and for a few good moments, taking a hard, deep look at myself.

The recovery process does not happen alone. One must examine and discard old habits and learn the basics all over again. An important part of that re-learning process is one's spiritual journey. The ancients refer to it as the core of one's true humanity and it begins through prayer or meditation. One must have a *base;* a spiritual connection to some *Thing,* a God Force in the universe that is greater than us, and which can provide us balance and who can help us hold things together. It is that close connection to God or some other universal force that the Twelve Step folks identify as one's Higher Power. This is where you will begin to feel a sense of comfort and inner peace as you face your personal demons while in recovery. This process should not be ignored. Welcome to the other side.

The point of all this is to stop, be still and reflect. Look deeply into the mirror of your soul and record what you see. Soon it will become easier to learn how to manage your recovery. Remember that your recovery must be earned. It will require that you do the work and give it all you've got. A great book that can help you through this is, *Now That You're Sober* by Earnie Larsen, a great speaker and recovery coach. It is a week-by-week guide for young people who are bravely moving through their first year of recovery. Read it and then read it again. Good material takes longer to digest. It's all good!

Here's an honest truth: *Getting sober is easy. Staying sober is the hard part.* If it seems like all the details and responsibilities you put on hold when went to rehab are now hitting you in the face and demanding your immediate attention, don't panic. What's most helpful now is to learn how to prioritize and to do only those things that are most beneficial to your sobriety. Recovery happens in stages and the road can often be filled with potholes and ruts. As Earnie Larsen so eloquent put it: *"Old habits die hard, so it becomes easy to rely on what has worked in the past be it good or bad."* I say some habits never die. They just lie in your path (as ruts) waiting for a moment to trip you up. I also say that change is difficult and testing new behaviors can wear a person down. Don't give in to old habits. The key to getting more acclimated to recovery is to learn how to take things in stride, one day at a time. Not everything that comes along today needs your attention. Put off what you can and concentrate on your recovery needs. As you begin to feel more at home doing what you need to for your sobriety, you will be able to devote the proper attention to other concerns. To modify a quote from Dr. Phil, *"You have the duty and gift of living. You don't have the right to sit on the sidelines just because you've made a mistake. You got your life back, now use it. Get back into the game."*

WHOLE LIFE RECOVERY

"You're the only thing in your way."
(Cloud Cult)

What I'm about to teach you is not hocus pocus. It's the real deal. Native cultures and modern day shamans teach that we are all a part of *one* natural system and that an individual's life is whole when it is in harmony with that system. Our life is made up of five critical life elements that play a reciprocal role with human behavior. They include the *physical, mental, emotional, social* and *spiritual*. It is the combination of these four life elements that work together to revitalize and balance a person's body and life's energies. People who exhibit these five life elements are referred to as *whole* beings. Achieving and maintaining balance within these five essential life elements provides us with a framework for healthy, purposeful living. Supporters of comprehensive, addiction aftercare refer to this philosophy as Whole Life Recovery. The recovering individual, then, is said to also be in a state of change; ever evolving from a state of active addiction to a state of physical, mental, intellectual, social and spiritual wellness. The recovering individual's main goal is to keep all five elements balanced and in check.

Recall for one moment when you were living the using life. You abandoned your critical life elements for drugs and alcohol. You neglected your health, you weren't making the right choices, you cheated and lied to yourself and to those you loved, and you abandoned your Higher Power. Now you must work to get those life elements back.

Imagine for a moment that our body is like an automobile with four tires and a steering wheel:

Physical **Mental** **Emotional** **Social** **Spiritual**

The tires and the steering wheel represent five life elements needed to guide us on life's journey, in this case, sobriety. Just like in an automobile, in order to ensure a safe journey ahead, we must keep our tires in check and balanced and our hands on the wheel at all times. In life, we must heal, develop, learn to make better choices and keep all life elements in check and well-balanced if we are to experience a positive recovery journey and a well-balanced life.

Building Recovery Capital in Our Five Life Elements

- The **physical.** The physical element refers to the physical body (brain included); the biological aspect of addiction and possibly addiction's first casualty. When addiction becomes the focus of one's life, hygiene suffers, and one's life becomes dominated by cravings. As the immune system becomes compromised, some people experience near-death experiences while others actually die.

  Our task as recovery coaches is to guide our clients through a process of exploring ways of building recovery capital in the physical element by taking back their good health and maintaining stability through physical care.

143

There are some who don't normally think of exercise as being important to recovery, but those who get in the habit of exercising report that it energizes them in ways they never could have predicted. And for some, exercise has certain spiritual qualities that seem to enhance other areas of their lives such as greater emotional balance and mental growth.

- The **mental** or cognitive element is comprised of our ability to think and reason, and consists of our thoughts, beliefs, and values. It is the foundation with which recovery coaching is built. In living a drug-induced lifestyle, the recovering person's mind became hijacked by drugs of choice which distorted his thinking capabilities. You could say that his recovery capital had become depleted and was kept in a perpetual state of confusion. His thinking became irrational and choices became limited. Couple this with values being out of sync with reality, and one can see the horrendous personal, spiritual, social and legal problems that addiction can cause. Our recovery has become depleted.

Through recovery coaching, clients are taught numerous ways of building recovery capital by challenging their distorted thinking patterns and beliefs, and to make reality checks until challenging and fact-checking becomes habit. As minds become clearer, clients become stronger and can better understand that their former addiction cannot define who they are as individuals and that each has the inner capacity to adopt new and healthier ways of looking at the world. This cognitive element always maintains a look toward the future and how to build a better life. This element will be discussed in detail as we proceed.

- The **emotional** element is about feeling and experiencing life in deep ways. It is the part of us that seeks meaningful contact with others. In living a drug-induced lifestyle, the recovering individual gave up on or avoided all contact with those he valued and loved. Waking hours were spent courting the obsession most loved: alcohol or drugs. The truth became blurred or lost as lies and false justifications were made. Lying, cheating, stealing and distorting the truth became a necessary part of the addictive process. The slippery slope to relapse always seems to begin with some form of dishonesty and self-deception. Fresh out of treatment (or jail), many recovering clients find themselves in a transition mode and burdened by the guilt and shame caused by their using behaviors and have no means or direction as to how to forgive themselves and pursue the forgiveness of those they have harmed. In order to make progress in recovery one needs to have what the prevention experts call a *transformation of character;* attitude adjustment. As our values and attitudes change, we change; and by changing, we build up recovery capital that strengthens and transforms us as we better able to forgive ourselves and begin asking those we hurt when we were living the using life for forgiveness. Through recovery coaching, clients can once again begin rebuild their self-confidence and work at regaining the trust of those they had once lost through alcohol and drugs.

- The **Social** element consists of activities that promote wellness within the client's circle: family & others. We usually begin using substances with other people and become part of social culture that has as its foundation addictive behaviors.

Recovery is about moving into a new mental state; a new neighborhood if you will that has in it a culture of new shared values that are positive and support sobriety and enhances well-being. It is about building caring relationships with others and engaging in activities that promote social capital.

- The **spiritual** element is one's steering wheel and is the domain of our soul that steers us in the right direction much like our moral compass. It is (or should be) a part of who we are. It is that place that extends beyond time and space; the "who am I and why am I here" part of life. It is not necessarily a religion, but it can be. It is a spiritual centeredness within us that says that we are a small part of some *thing* greater than us; that we belong. While living the drug-induced lifestyle, the addicted person became disconnected from his Higher Power; the Great Spirit; God and lost his purpose in life. The A.A. folks refer to it as being *spiritually bankrupt;* a loss of connection to one's Higher Power. Spiritually bankrupt people have, in essence, lost their moral compass, and as a result of their poor choices, will soon veer off the path and wind up in a ditch.

Balance is the Challenge

The point that whole life recovery makes to people is: if *disconnection* from all five life elements was a problem while addicted, then shouldn't *reconnection* be the solution now that you are in recovery? Drugs and alcohol serve to isolate us, not only from our Creator, but from friends and family.

Think back. As your addiction took hold you spent more time with those who let you drink and drug as much as you liked. You begin to avoid those who love you and who expressed concern about your behavior. You also began to avoid God. Drugs and alcohol have failed to fill the void you felt. But back in your mind (or your heart), you knew something was very wrong.

Now that your head is clear, you are beginning to connect the dots. You want to feel part of something bigger; reconnect with things and people you love. Spiritual thinkers across all religions and traditions have taught that our bodies are a temple and that life is about moving forward, not backward. They taught that in order for humans to live productive lives; the totality of mind, body, and spirit must be nurtured, appreciated and kept in balance in the context of the moment.

That's all I've got to say, my friend. There is only one way to truly heal your life and find peace, and that is through recovery and reconnection. But you can't do it alone. God, your Higher Power is there to take the burden and carry you when you can't do it yourself. So if you have disconnected yourself from the five life elements through addiction, then doesn't it make sense to try and regain what was lost in that disconnection and become whole once again? Paste this final quotation on your refrigerator and read it each day before you walk out the door: *In recovery, balance is the challenge.* Again, welcome to the other side.

ABOUT STARTING POINT

Who We Are and What We Do

Starting Point offers clients in their first year of recovery a strengths-based support mechanism that is founded on the principle that every individual has the internal resources and inherent capacity to transform their lives. We empower our clients to build on their successes and find ways to stop the relapse cycle. Starting Point helps those in recovery who feel they lack direction or fear recovery success. We provide the skills needed to tear down the external and internal walls that prevent recovery persons from meeting their own needs and goals. We teach self-empowerment and self-reliance as our clients learn the elements of *Whole Life Recovery* and how to properly manage their lives and the challenges of re-entering a sober world. Our coaching program works because it is easy for clients to understand; it makes sense, and it gets results.

Starting Point offers a comprehensive six-point plan on how to:

- Manage irrational, addictive thinking and beliefs.
- Manage addictive feelings.
- Manage self-defeating addictive behaviors.
- Manage anger in recovery.
- Develop a personal relapse prevention plan.
- Whole Life Recovery: Creating a sober-for-life standard of living.

Client Training Format:

- Intake interview to set goals, and outline program expectations.
- Ninety day client commitment.
- A combination of in-class and home-study model.
- Skype self-reporting and follow-up.
- A Certificate of Completion provided upon training completion.

Client Training Topics:

- Self-deception, justification, and faulty thinking.
- Straight thinking: managing addictive thinking and feelings.
- Managing anger while in recovery
- Solutions-based thinking.
- Restructuring self-sabotaging thoughts and behaviors.
- Recognizing relapse triggers and implementing solution-based strategies.
- Responsible life skills: Stepping away from the revolving door.

LITERARY RESOURCES

I would like to thank those whose works inspired me throughout this project and who not only contributed thoughts, theories and notions, but gave their kind permission to use excerpts from their works. They include: Staff members at Al-Anon Family Group Headquarters, Alcoholics Anonymous, New Beginnings at Waverly, Partnership for a Drug-Free America and Relate Counseling Center of Minnesota.

I would also like to acknowledge the contributions of various persons in the addiction recovery field notably: Evolution Recovery House, Hazelden, Lighthouse Mission Ministries and the works of Beverly Conyers, Eric Mayo, and Melodie Beattie, whose excerpts I used to drive home key points. This is by no means an exhaustive list of resources, but the following books and web sites were useful in the preparation of this book. They include:

- *The Purpose Driven Life: What On Earth Am I Here For.* Rick Warren.
- *Motivational Enhancement Therapy with Drug Abusers.* William R. Miller, Ph.D.
- *The Enabler.* Angelyn Miller.
- *Starting Recovery with Relapse Prevention.* Terence T. Gorski
- *The Dance of Wounded Souls.* Robert Burney
- *Now That You're Sober.* Earnie Larsen with Carol Larsen Hegarty.
- *Alcoholics Anonymous Big Book Vol. 4.* AA Services.
- *Don't Let Your Kids Kill you*; A guide for parents of drug and alcohol addicted children. Charles Rubin.
- Lauren Wispé. *The Psychology of Sympathy.*
- *Bodies in Motion and at Rest.* Thomas Lynch.
- *Save My Son.* Maralys Wills and Mike Carona.
- *Recovery of Chemical Dependent Families (booklet)*: Hazelden.
- *Preventing Adolescent Relapse.* Tammy Bell
- *Beautiful Boy.* David Sheff
- *Your Erroneous Zone.* Wayne Dyer.
- *Addict in the Family.* Beverly Conyers.

- *Everything Changes: Help for Families of Newly Recovering Addicts.* Beverly Conyers.
- *Become a Better You:* Joel Osteen
- *Portrait of an Addict as a Young Man.* Bill Clegg.
- *Ties That Bind: A self-Help Guide to Change Through Family of Origin Therapy.* Ronald W. Richardson.
- *Letters to a Young Brother.* Hill Harper.
- *When God Stopped Keeping Score.* R.A.Clark.
- *Co-dependent No More.* Melodie Beattie.

- *The Language of Letting Go.* Melodie Beattie.
- *Addiction.* HBO Series. (2005)
- *Recovery of Chemical Dependent Families.* (booklet). Hazelden/Johnson Institute, 1987.
- *National Institute on Drug Abuse for Teens.* www.teens.drugabuse.gov
- *Crime and Punishment in America.* Elliott Currie, 1998.

(Subtitle quotations and song excerpts used with gratitude: Sarah McLachlan, Joel Osteen, Amy Winehouse, The Grateful Dead, The Eagles, Foo Fighters, Cloud Cult, Al-Anon, Sly and the Family Stone, George Harrison, Jefferson Airplane, Bob Dylan Alcoholics Anonymous, and the Wounded Soul Project.)

www.ingramcontent.com/pod-product-compliance
Lightning Source LLC
Chambersburg PA
CBHW070916290526
45795CB00001B/336